CW00816136

THE FOUND VOICE

THE FOUND VOICE

VOICE

WRITERS' BEGINNINGS

DENIS SAMPSON

OXFORD
UNIVERSITY PRESS

OXFORD
UNIVERSITY PRESS

Great Clarendon Street, Oxford, OX2 6DP,
United Kingdom

Oxford University Press is a department of the University of Oxford.
It furthers the University's objective of excellence in research, scholarship,
and education by publishing worldwide. Oxford is a registered trade mark of
Oxford University Press in the UK and in certain other countries

© Denis Sampson 2016

The moral rights of the author have been asserted

First Edition published in 2016

Impression: 1

Published in the United States of America by Oxford University Press
198 Madison Avenue, New York, NY 10016, United States of America

British Library Cataloguing in Publication Data
Data available

Library of Congress Control Number: 2015951895

ISBN 978–0–19–875299–8

Printed in Great Britain by
Clays Ltd, St Ives plc

For Gay

Acknowledgements

I am indebted to editors of journals who invited me to contribute and then published early versions of some of this work: Douglas Archibald, editor, *Colby Quarterly*, 'William Trevor: Notes for an Unwritten Biography'; Emmanuel Vernadakis, editor, *Journal of the Short Story in English*, 'Mavis Gallant's "Voices Lost in Snow": The Origins of Fiction'; Boris Castel, editor, *Queen's Quarterly*, 'Mavis Gallant and the Authentic Voices of the Dead'; and Maurice Earls, editor, the *Dublin Review of Books* (www.drb.ie), 'Belonging and Becoming' (on the memoir fictions of J. M. Coetzee).

I have made extensive use of libraries: the Social Sciences and Humanities Library of McGill University, Montreal; the Vanier Library, Concordia University, Montreal; the Lecky Library of Trinity College, Dublin. My friend Adrian King-Edwards, bookseller, gave me access to his rich collection of early and rare editions when I was working on the Gallant and Munro chapters. While I have also made extensive use of sites on the Internet, especially for retrieving interviews and other material that would otherwise remain inaccessible, the printed books on the library shelves and on my own shelves were of primary importance.

Mid way through the writing of this book, I realized that it may have had its origins some decades ago in the words of Louis Dudek, eminent poet, critic, and professor at McGill University. When he joined my PhD supervisory committee late, he read my draft and asked 'But where is *your* voice?' His words made all the difference. Sadly, my thanks to Louis Dudek has to be a posthumous one. Two critical books found on the shelves also had an indirect but sustaining influence: James Olney's *Metaphors of Self: The Meaning of Autobiography* (Princeton, NJ, 1972) and Francis-Noël Thomas's *The Writer Writing: Philosophic Acts in Literature* (Princeton, NJ, 1992). During the writing of this book, I had regular conversations with my friend Bryan Doubt, whose lifelong work with actors on voice and text had nourished his interest in articulating something similar in his field to what I have attempted here. His constant interest over these past years sustained many pleasurable conversations and the energy that flowed from them.

I am indebted to Jacqueline Baker at OUP, who encouraged me to undertake this book, and to the two anonymous readers whose keen interest had an inspiring and energizing effect. Their comments led to considerable improvement in the quality of argument and the overall shape of major parts of the book. I thank both of them for making this a much better book than it might otherwise have been.

Once again, it is a pleasure to acknowledge the help of Jonathan Williams, whose unerring eye for blunders in all textual matters has become my safety net. More than that, his extraordinary commitment to good writing and to the literary life is deeply sustaining and deserves wider recognition than these few words here can offer.

Contents

Prologue

The writing voice

In this set of essays on V. S. Naipaul, Alice Munro, William Trevor, Mavis Gallant, and J. M. Coetzee, my intention is to focus on a crucial moment in the formation of their artistic identities. I want to map the first discovery by each of these major writers of their own free and distinct creative self. In the case of each artist, the writing of a pivotal novel or set of stories released a liberating power that carried them beyond the apprenticeship stage. Inhibiting literary means and styles were surmounted, and a clarity of purpose and style became possible; simultaneously, they came to recognize and accept their own material, out of which they could elaborate a unique fictional universe. My intention is to identify the original energies and artistic goals that fused at this moment, and to outline ways in which that synthesis became a foundation for much of their subsequent individual careers.

V. S. Naipaul reflected many times on his literary beginnings, and in his essay 'Reading and Writing', he speaks of the discovery of his material, 'the city street [in Port of Spain] from whose mixed life we had held aloof, and the country life before that, with the ways and manners of a remembered India'.[1] Leaving Trinidad to study at Oxford, he had expected that he would find his material in England and become an 'English' writer, so this discovery came as a surprise to him. 'Almost at the same time came the language, the tone, the voice for the material,' he writes. 'It was as if voice and matter and form were part of one another.'[2] He says that 'the voice in my head' was to some extent that of his father in his stories of the displaced Indian community and in part the anonymous voice of a mid-sixteenth-century Spanish story he had translated, but his 'writing voice' is more than an imitated style copied from these sources, something he admits in speaking of what he 'had worked hard to find'.

'Finding a voice' is a common metaphoric phrase writers rely on to suggest an ability that was not available to them earlier: 'People like me write,' William Trevor has said, 'because otherwise we are pretty inarticulate. Our articulation is our writing.'[3] Not all my subjects are as interested as Naipaul in creating a narrative of their beginnings, but in their references to this new power, almost invariably they associate it with voice. J. M. Coetzee has spoken of a long preparation before he began to write fiction, but during that time, he had 'literary ambitions' to 'speak one day in [my] own voice', and he will later refer to 'the voice of the mind, the voice in the mind'.[4] For poets and some novelists too, the phrase is useful because it draws attention to a distinctive style that is grounded in an oral or physical quality, even, to a degree, in a local dialect. That is a notable feature of Coetzee's first novel, *Dusklands*, which experiments with many dramatized narrators—all unreliable—and is centrally preoccupied with the authenticity of the artistic voice, especially in repressive political and historical contexts, such as South Africa. Although many writers accept a moral imperative to 'give voice' to an obscured or marginalized community that has shaped them, 'voice' is not to be confused here with 'speaking out' in public. In Coetzee's case, for instance, his scrupulous conscience regarding the appropriate voice of the confessional self anchors his work in literary traditions that question the authenticity of many notions of selfhood and cultural identity.

The expression 'finding a voice' also refers to the way a writing self discovers itself, or locates itself 'among the voices' of literary tradition. Mavis Gallant said with reference to her own stories, 'If I read a passage aloud, I am conscious of a prose rhythm easy for me to follow, that must be near to the way I think and speak.'[5] Gallant commented very rarely on specific stories, but she was forthright in what she claimed for their provenance. 'There is no such thing as a writer who has escaped being influenced' by the classic status of earlier writers, she declared, yet inspiring influences must be worked through: 'Style cannot be copied, except by the untalented. . . . if it is not a true voice, it is nothing.'[6] The voice that Gallant hears when she reads a passage of her work is the 'true voice' that she has distilled from her reading and her own self-definition. Having found her material, 'only personal independence matters' to the beginning writer, she insists, quoting Pasternak.[7]

In the intimate, private space of creation, writers are inclined to value their freedom to experiment. 'The *feel* of writing fiction,' Coetzee remarks, 'is one of freedom, of irresponsibility, or better, of responsibility toward something that has not yet emerged, that lies somewhere at the end of the road.'[8] Trevor, surprisingly, expresses this more forcefully: 'I think all writing is experimental. The very obvious sort of experimental writing is not really more experimental than that of a conventional writer like myself.'[9] In this sense, writers may not wish to be limited in their artistic work to the role of historical witness or spokesperson, or to the duties and responsibilities of autobiographer, nor do they want to be called on to explain or comment on aspects of their work. Alice Munro remarks, 'I am not concerned with using what is real to make any sort of record or prove any sort of point, and I am not concerned with any methods of selection but my own, which I can't fully explain.'[10] Naipaul, Gallant, Munro, and Trevor all emphasize this intuitive compass that located their distinctive creative direction and kept them on course. If artistic intuition is an elusive force for biographers to trace, it is, nevertheless, the writer's confidence in its reliability and truth that grounds the writing of that special book.

This intuitive sense that guides the writing with such confidence is related to the inner voice, and this, in turn, appears to be related to memory as much as observation. Coetzee identifies 'chance, memory and introspection' as the origins of a writer's material, even in the case of one with strong links to realism or naturalism. Although Naipaul drew on memories of childhood in Port of Spain for *Miguel Street* and other fiction, surprisingly, towards the end of his career, he identified Proust as a touchstone. In closing his Nobel lecture, he reaffirms the 'intuitive way in which I have written' and then quotes Proust: 'Those who are obsessed by this blurred memory of truths they have never known are the men who are gifted. . . . Talent is like a sort of memory which will enable them finally to bring this indistinct music closer to them, to hear it clearly, to note it down.'[11] Proust's linking of involuntary memory and imagination—here it is referred to not as voice in language but as heard music—has also touched Trevor: 'A huge amount of what I write about is internal, a drifting back into childhood, based on a small event or a moment.'[12] All these writers, in fact, acknowledge that even if their material is partially drawn from recollected scenes, places, and characters, from images, more important is the way the deepest memories are released into the writing voice.

In order to become able to articulate a distinctive style, each of them had to overcome specific personal and cultural circumstances, and to free themselves from inherited or earlier ways of thinking and writing.[13] And yet their complex bond to that inheritance became their material. Most of my subjects grew up isolated from the cultural mainstream of their homeland, alienated even, and desperate to define their place. Naipaul has written novels, historical essays, and memoirs which explore over and over the precarious place of his Hindu ancestors in the mixed-race culture of Trinidad, while Coetzee has explored with extraordinary intensity the burden of his Afrikaans inheritance. Montreal was the first home of Mavis Gallant; she was sent to French schools, but when her family disintegrated, she was brought to the United States, where she spent her adolescence; at eighteen, she returned independently to the city, lived there, and worked in English for most of a decade before moving permanently to Europe in 1950, eventually settling in Paris. William Trevor grew up in a series of towns in Ireland, an Anglican on the margins of the predominantly Catholic and nationalist culture, although not privileged or descended from the former colonial establishment; he did not feel at home in either community. Like so many of his compatriots, Trevor moved to Britain to find work, which he did as a sculptor and teacher and then in an advertising agency in London, before turning to writing. Although Alice Munro did not leave Canada, she left her childhood home near a small town in Ontario at the age of twenty and moved four thousand kilometres to the city of Vancouver; as in the case of Trevor, uprooting and resettling appears to have left Munro with the imaginative challenge of observing the new and, a decade later, needing to discover how to re-envisage in maturity the society she had left, and to which she eventually returned.

The personal circumstances are different in each case, some more estranging, disruptive, and irrevocable than others. Sooner or later, all found imaginative freedom and a deeper engagement in their art by turning inward and back, some by inventing versions of an earlier, lost, home. In moving away and finding a place in another culture, they realized that they had become foreign to themselves and must go beyond that condition to make a virtue of necessity. Unlike many of the masters of modernism, such as Joyce or Nabokov, they do not identify exile as a defining condition, nor do they follow the postmodernist Beckett, who ruminated endlessly on selfhood and estrangement:

'What would I say if I had a voice, who is this, saying it's me?'[14] In order to bring their place of origin back into a meaningful focus, their material for fiction, they had to discover a method and style for seeing earlier experience from a migrant's perspective. They had to discover a writing voice that would reconcile them to the disparate experiences of their own estranged condition and would allow them to develop with a more confident sense of their integrity and independence as artists.

I

V. S. Naipaul's *Miguel Street*
The 'first true book'

In 'Prologue to an Autobiography' V. S. Naipaul includes an extended account of how his 'first true book' came to him in the early summer of 1955. In that 'narrative' and in many interviews over the decades, he refers to *Miguel Street*, a collection of linked stories, as his first publishable book, although it was not the first published. Having set himself the goal of becoming a novelist at an early age, he completed two novels before writing, at the age of twenty-three, the first work of fiction he felt was 'true'. This characterization of *Miguel Street* actually comes from an account written in 1993, ten years after 'Prologue', in the 'sequence' *A Way in the World*. There is another, brief, account of its composition in the 'novel' *The Enigma of Arrival*, in a section called 'The Journey'; and there are others: in the novel *Half a Life*, in 'Reading and Writing', in his Nobel Prize address, and in *A Writer's People: Ways of Looking and Feeling*. Clearly, this idea of a unique kind of beginning, and of a 'true book', have assumed mythological significance in Naipaul's interpretation of his own evolution as a writer; even more, it seems that he defines many of his aims and later accomplishments as an artist by reference to this moment in 1955.

Writing the first account of what happened was not easy, and the number of times Naipaul felt the need to include a retelling in later fictions and essays is surely striking. 'Prologue' was first published in *Finding the Centre* in 1983, along with an extended travel 'narrative' about a stay in West Africa, and the brief preface to that book makes clear that 'the centre' is what his literary enterprise attempts to find in all its various journeys, geographical and autobiographical. More than this, he says he wants to 'admit the reader' to 'the process of writing', to his own 'centre' as an artist. The preface also tells that he had first considered an investigation of the background to the writing of *Miguel Street* in 1967, and again in 1972 and in 1977, but it was only in 1982 that he was able to find the 'narrative' of his beginnings as a writer.[1] Finally, he came to believe that he had found his own 'centre', but two other narratives are integral to the partial autobiography: a meditation on his father's fragile identity as a writer on the margins of the Indian community in Trinidad and an exploration of the man nicknamed Bogart, a cousin, equally marginalized in the multi-racial colony, both of whom obsess Naipaul as emblems of that cultural and historical condition.

He begins with an account of how 'Bogart', the opening story of *Miguel Street*, came to be written. One afternoon in the BBC freelance room in London, already almost five years away from Trinidad, Naipaul typed the sentence: 'Every morning when he got up Hat would sit on the banister of his back verandah and shout across, "What happening there, Bogart?" '[2] This sentence came spontaneously, as he tells it, and was quickly followed by another, and Naipaul describes how he did not leave the typewriter until the whole story was complete. Some kind of 'magic' was working, and the physical act of writing, the inner state, and the narrative style coincided in a lucky event: 'Luck was with me, because that first sentence was so direct, so uncluttered, so without complications, that it provoked the sentence that was to follow. . . . The first sentence was true. The second was invention. But together—to me, the writer—they had done something extraordinary.'[3] The 'world of the street' which is brought to life poetically and dramatically in this and the stories that followed day by day is, in fact, a particular kind of male, street community, each individual known primarily in the public space and so remaining to a degree masked or mysterious.

This cultural space is woven partly of memories from periods in Naipaul's childhood and youth when he moved from the countryside to live with his extended family on Luis Street in Port of Spain— 'things barely remembered, things released only by the act of writing', he says later.[4] Impressionistic memories are supplemented by material taken from films, city folklore, and songs of the 1930s and 1940s when he had lived there.[5] His young narrator, unlike himself when he first lived in Port of Spain, is very close to the men on the street, sharing their culture and sometimes participating in the storyline, so that, to a degree, the stories tell themselves and are free of retrospective commentary, explanation, or judgement. Naipaul captures a local culture with an intimate, 'insider' view—the 'centre' of that Trinidadian urban experience of migrating, mixed-race populations. The fiction he invented is more intuitive than sociological, more imaginative recreation than reportage; it is 'true' not only to what he observed and remembered but to his own identity as observer.

The typescript (completed, he says, in five or six weeks) made its way, with the help of a colleague on the BBC programme 'Caribbean Voices', to the hands of Diana Athill, who accepted it for publication at André Deutsch with great enthusiasm. Deutsch decided, however, that he would publish the stories only if Naipaul could submit an acceptable novel. Naipaul wrote *The Mystic Masseur* in a matter of months, and it, together with another novel, *The Suffrage of Elvira*, appeared before *Miguel Street*. These three works of fiction of his Trinidad experience, and, in particular, of the Hindu background of the Indian migrant community of his family, were followed by *A House for Mister Biswas*, and it might be said that these four books all grew out of that first sentence of the story 'Bogart'. Athill, and the British reading public which the books found, were receptive to writing that was outside the mainstream fiction of British social life, the most successful exponent of it in the mid-1950s being Evelyn Waugh. Athill brought onto her list in the mid-1950s novelists such as Mordecai Richler, writing of Jewish Montreal, and Brian Moore, writing of Belfast, both, like Naipaul, hailing from 'the colonies' although they did not write with an imperial/colonial perspective. Andrew Salkey, the freelance who brought *Miguel Street* to Athill, knew of her partiality to such writing, and in this Naipaul was doubly lucky, but, in fact, as he looks back at this time, he is aware that it is not the close-up treatment of Caribbean material, its exoticism, or its ethnographic accuracy, or, indeed its implicit anti-imperial politics, that interest him; it is the voice he found which allowed him to confidently bring its centre to life.[6]

This definitive 'beginning' in his writing of fiction created a persona and released an energy that carried Naipaul through the first phase of his career. In retrospect, it became the foundation of a myth of his own identity as a writer, not only as a novelist but as a travel writer and autobiographer. Over many decades, as the boundaries between fiction and non-fiction blurred, the character of the writer/observer/narrator became central to the travel books on India and many other places and to other kinds of semi-autobiographical narratives, such as

The Enigma of Arrival and *A Way in the World*. He returned to investigate this moment of 'illumination' as a discovery of an authentic style, but it also became a measure of the authenticity of his creative commitment to 'truth' over his lifetime, the truth of what he saw in the world and the truth of his way of seeing.

There is a specificity to writing. Certain settings, certain cultures, have to be written about in a certain way. These ways are not interchangeable.... It is the better and truer part of the labour of a writer from a new place to work out what his material is, to wring substance from the unwritten about and unregarded local scene.[7]

It may be that the 'centre' he articulated in writing about the composition of 'Bogart' identified the challenge that remained central to the whole career: how to successfully find a style for each world he observed and for the self that observed it.

Naipaul observed Luis Street for the first time in 1938, when, at age six, he moved with his parents from the compound of his maternal grandmother in the country town of Chiguanas to a house that she had bought in the capital. His recollection of his vantage-point is significant: 'My grandmother's house stood on tallish concrete pillars. To stand beside the banisters on the steps gave a perfect view of the street and the people. I got to know the people well, though I never spoke to them and they never spoke to me. I got to know their clothes and style and voices.'[8] In *A Writer's People*, Naipaul emphasizes the earlier experience of arrival in Port of Spain, but in his Nobel address, entitled 'Two Worlds', he is more explicit: 'There was no big corrugated-iron gate shutting out the world there. The life of the street was open to me. It was an intense pleasure for me to observe it from the verandah.'[9] The 'perfect view' was a curious child's way of knowing, safely, without direct involvement, and yet the heightened power of observation and later recall suggest that there was an intensity in the child's experience similar to what other writers have associated with an artistic way of seeing, with wonder and before judgement or explanation enter in. The 'two worlds' are not then simply the confined and ritualized Indian family set off against the mixed-race world of the street; they are the world of order and knowledge, associated later with writing, versus the disorder of the world of migration, of cultural confusion, and historical sequences of dispossession and imperial power. As a child, Naipaul felt the schism between the two worlds, and was taught to keep them apart as far as possible, but it seems that from his earliest years the bridging of the gap was his desire and ambition, to overcome estrangement. His arrival on Luis Street, commemorated in a sense in *Miguel Street*, gave him his first opportunity to attempt a reconciliation of self and the surrounding world.

What he absorbed at that age was overlaid, however, by another set of memories because the family moved away after a year or two to another country compound of his maternal grandmother. Isolated and cut off once more, he spent a few years there before they returned to Luis Street. Naipaul was an adolescent then, attended secondary school, moved out into the city, and mingled with the general population. He worked briefly in an office before setting off for London shortly before his eighteenth birthday. The experiences of this later time and the types of curiosity and observation that he developed as he matured were of a different kind and, to a degree, add a more 'knowing' layer to the depiction of the multifarious lives on the street. In recalling the way in which the stories came to him in the BBC room, he does not distinguish between the earlier and later observations and generally conveys the idea that he wrote out of the earlier experience, at the age of six or seven, although his narrator ages through adolescence until he leaves Trinidad.

During the second period of residence on Luis Street, the studious boy attended Queen's Royal College. There he was exposed to the traditional canon of English literature. For his scholarship studies for university in England, however, he chose to concentrate on French and Spanish literature. His father admired Shakespeare and Dickens, Maugham and O. Henry and de Maupassant, and read extracts to his son. As a self-educated man, Seepersad Naipaul's enthusiasms included the popular fiction of the time and also writing from India—epics, legends, and supernatural tales—and Gandhi's *Autobiography*, all of which he shared with his adolescent son. But young Naipaul's ambition to be a writer was not furthered in a practical way by much of this reading: 'The effect was to introduce me to the romantic idea of this world outside, and to the romantic idea of writing.'[10] Apart from Dickens, perhaps, he did not find in these books a model for his own work.

His father was a working journalist, an observer of topical and contemporary events, and at an early age, Naipaul kept journals, in which he noted down his own observations. At sixteen he began to contribute sketches and reviews to magazines, and, in spite of his later insistence on his provincial ignorance and insecurity, it is clear that he was already a precocious and disciplined writer. In the year or so between winning his scholarship and actually leaving Trinidad, he had time to write:

I had nothing to write about: I was just preparing to be a writer. . . . Sometimes I wrote descriptions of landscapes: the Petit Valley woods, remnants of old cocoa estates in the hills to the north-west of the city, after afternoon rain. Sometimes I did Port of Spain scenes: the Western Main Road in St James at night, after rain (more rain), the red neon Coca-Cola sign on the Rialto cinema flicking on and off. . . Artificial, but everything I worked on in this way stayed with me, and years later some of those descriptions were to be a key to events and moods I had thought beyond recall.[11]

He was aware, however, that there was no indigenous tradition of writing about Trinidad; it had been written about by European visitors, and he concludes later that he had deep underlying 'doubts' already about his own ability to actually understand the significance of what he saw.

Yet he was even more ambitious and began a novel: 'At that time of optimism between leaving school and waiting to go to England and Oxford, I had started . . . a novel, a farce with a local setting.'[12] It was, he said late in life, 'much influenced by Evelyn Waugh'. He continued to work on it in Oxford and completed it two years later, in the summer of 1951. By then his first stories had just been broadcast on the BBC's 'Caribbean Voices', and he was hopeful that the novel would be published, but he was disappointed. Later, he regularly dismissed the apprentice work as fatally undermined by the 'uncertainty of his writing personality'.[13] Only after 'vision was granted me' in writing *Miguel Street* would he accept that his fiction was 'true', and he implicitly erased this earlier work and would not allow any continuity between it and what came later.

The Enigma of Arrival includes an extended account of various attempts at this time to write fiction based on observations of people Naipaul encountered on his journey by sea to London and during his first months in the city. Essentially he characterizes these efforts as a misguided attempt to find 'suitable metropolitan material' and to display 'a particular kind of writing personality', akin to Maugham, Waugh or Aldous Huxley. 'Gala Night' was based on experiences on board ship, but in retrospect, he emphasizes how he had failed to use the people and events that were of significance in signposting the changes he himself was undergoing: the departure from his family, his growing self-consciousness about race, meeting other migrating individuals. 'Thinking of myself as a writer, I was hiding my experience from myself; hiding myself from my experience.'[14] In England, he worked on a piece called 'Angela', based on his relationship with the manager of a boarding house in Earl's Court who befriended him, and another, 'Life in London', inspired by passing contact with the management couple who were about to leave the boarding house. Naipaul uses his account of these fictions and the circumstances they were based on to advance an argument about his stage of development during these years, an imaginative paralysis owing to a crippling awareness of con-flicting selves. 'Man' and 'writer' were separated when he left Trinidad, and it took many years until they could be reconciled in the writing of *Miguel Street*.

In late 1954, after he left Oxford for London, he began a new novel that he characterizes as an exercise in 'introversion'. Contrasting it with the farce of the earlier Trinidad novel, he writes in *A Way in the World* that it was 'something very serious', based on 'someone like myself, working as a clerk in the Registrar-general's office in Port of Spain', but 'all I could think of in the way of narrative was a day in the life of this character'.[15] He had a title, 'The Shadow'd Livery', taken from *The Merchant of Venice*, 'Mislike me not for my complexion...', which suggests that his subject was race. Almost forty years later, he writes with distaste about his younger self and his attempt to write a novel:

I didn't know what attitude to take to the character or the setting. I couldn't see it clearly.... Writing should have helped me to see, to clarify myself; but every day as I wrote my novel (when I wasn't doing little things for money at the BBC), the fabrication, the turning away from the truths I couldn't fully acknowledge, pressed me down further into the little hole I had created for myself.[16]

These years in Oxford and London, as his ambition weighed on him and he tried to situate himself socially, were marked by seriously depressive periods. He felt he had failed to find his subject or his own style.

'The Shadow'd Livery' was the novel he showed to Arthur Calder Marshall in spring 1955. Although Calder Marshall ('Foster Morris' in

A Way in the World), an English critic who had written a book about Trinidad, aimed to help, and offered advice, Naipaul 'felt dreadfully abased' by his rejection of the novel. In this state of humiliation, he may have allowed himself a few weeks to take stock of the fictional styles he had experimented with already, and in solitude to prepare for a 'fresh start': 'I thought I would turn away from what I had done, and go back to the beginning: try to see whether I couldn't make writing out of plain concrete statements, adding meaning to meaning in simple stages.'[17] That sounds like a reflection of the advice to study Hemingway's method, given him by 'Foster Morris'.

In *A Way in the World*, he adds a further scene to suggest how he returned to his earliest material to see it in a new light:

At tea in the BBC canteen one day we were talking about George Lamming's autobiography, *In the Castle of my Skin*. The producer [Henry Swanzy] wanted to talk only about a small comic episode in the book...I learned as a new truth what I had always known, and what so far in my writing (veering between farce and introversion) I had suppressed: that comedy, the preserver we in Trinidad had always known, was close to me, a double inheritance, from my story-telling Hindu family and from the creole street life of Port of Spain.[18]

The narratives of how Naipaul came to write *Miguel Street*, here and in *The Enigma of Arrival*, are certainly dramatized in ways that are appropriate to the larger patterns of those books, but this scene is surely a tribute to the influence of Henry Swanzy. Naipaul seems to credit him for the crucial shift in tone from farce to comedy, which he now sees as close to the centre of the style he discovered:

...the language discipline...the comedy. Together they had given me confidence; but they had also given me a writing character...the ability to make two or three jokes to the page, the jokeyness that was my double inheritance... however good, however illuminating, was also a way of making peace with a hard world; was on the other side of hysteria. This was true of the colonial society I was writing about; it was also true of my own position in London.[19]

It was finally through this detached, comic tone that observation and autobiographical feeling were integrated, that 'man' and 'writer' were reconciled in the sudden emergence of the new style and the writer's character. The expressions 'making peace with a hard world' and 'the other side of hysteria' give extraordinary force to the need that drove this breakthrough and suggest that the writing of 'Bogart' was a way of liberating himself from the alienation Naipaul had experienced in colonial Trinidad and, equally, from what he had encountered in his migration to Oxford and London.

Rejecting the poised writer-personalities of established English authors, some of whom had written about Trinidad or other colonies, Naipaul found a tone of attention and acceptance, a balancing of sympathy and distance, without satire, angry criticism, or political message. This balancing was something he needed for looking at the chaotic, colonial society, of which he felt his father was a victim, and of which he himself was fearful, and for freeing himself from the despair of his own depressive and conflicted self. The voice he was able to capture in the stories represented order and confidence in the face of the destructive forces he had encountered and internalized. The long apprenticeship to the vocation of writer through adolescence, his years as a student and then as a freelance in London came to an end. Writing *Miguel Street* gave him confidence in himself as author for the first time, and it did so in his discovery of an appropriate fictional method and voice for a place that he would see as if for the first time.

∿

'Bogart', the opening story, introduces the reader to a special world, the 'Club' of men on the street, and each story brings into focus a separate person, but there is a small chorus of people, led by Hat, who establish that focus. The narrator is, in a sense, observing and listening for himself but is also guided by Hat's comments. It is only in the penultimate story, 'Hat', that Hat's own life is brought into focus, and that story concludes 'When Hat went to jail, part of me had died.'[20] Many of the men end up in jail, including Bogart and Popo, introduced in the first story and the central character in the second; it almost seems like a rite of passage for these men. But what has died for the narrator is the part of him that relied on Hat as a guide: 'it was just three years, three years in which I had grown up and looked critically at the people around me.... Everything had changed.'[21] Embedded in the collection of stories, then, is an oblique investigation of the code of masculinity that, at first, the narrator accepts uncritically, but in the years covered by the stories, he grows up and apart from the culture of the street, and the final story is entitled 'How I Left Miguel Street'. The maturation of the narrator is not explicitly signalled to the reader until the end, but in fact, a part of the drama of the narrative perspective is that he is both 'innocent' and retrospectively 'knowing'. Looking 'critically' may be the mark of maturity, but the predominant tone is sympathy and acceptance because Naipaul's discovery was how to allow Hat and the street characters to be the narrators of their own lives.

The role of Hat in relation to the narrator is established right away. 'Every morning when he got up Hat would sit...,' and then, following Bogart's response, 'What happening there, Hat?' the narrator comments: 'It was something of a mystery why he was called Bogart; but I suspect that it was Hat who gave him the name.'[22] The migrant from the countryside who arrived to live intermittently on the street was first nicknamed 'Patience' because he spent long hours playing the solitary card-game. The young narrator had observed him: 'he looked so bored and superior', 'not a funny man', 'with a captivating languor', and while emphasizing the boredom, he finds 'a grace' in his movements. To begin with, he may have been captivated by 'the mystery' of this taciturn man, but an older voice intrudes: 'He made a pretence of making a living by tailoring'.[23] When 'hundreds of young men began adopting the hard-boiled Bogartian attitude' in the wake of the release of *Casablanca* in 1942, making 'a pretence' became a way of life. Bogart began to live up to the role Hat had given him, and more than this is implied in the opening page of the story: the street is a kind of stage on which the characters make occasional appearances, playing various roles, but their real lives are only glimpsed, the 'mystery' of each one preserved until suddenly they disappear or end up in jail, and facts of economic desolation or personal desperation take the place of fantasies. The naïve narrator is drawn into the fantasies, and there is no overt judgement of Hat when the facts are revealed.

The narrator is intrigued by Bogart, and by Hat's relationship with him. At first, when the man in the servant room was 'Patience', his quiet presence led to acceptance. 'It is still something of a miracle to me that Bogart managed to make friends', the narrator comments. 'He never told a story. Yet whenever there was a fête or something like that, everybody would say, "We must have Bogart. He smart like hell, that man." In a way, he gave them great solace and comfort, I suppose.'[24] But the 'man of mystery' who intrigues both Hat and the narrator 'vanished' one day: he 'left us without a word'. Some time later, he returns, changed: he has truly grown into the persona of Bogart: 'he had got it right. He was just like an actor.'[25] And he tells the 'story' of where he has been, in South America, running a brothel, until he was arrested. So arrogant is he in playing the role that the narrator notes that Hat's response is to adopt another film-star persona, that of Rex

Harrison. Bogart disappears twice more, until, eventually, a newspaper reports that he had been convicted of bigamy. The facts emerge that, rather than live out the plot of a film in British Guiana, as he had pretended, he had lived with two women in different parts of Trinidad, and had married and left both of them. It is Hat who tells the facts to the street, and when someone asks why Bogart left these women, Hat replies: 'To be a man among we men'.[26]

By the end of the book, the narrator is about to detach himself from Hat and from the world of the street, and it is significant that Naipaul delays the portrait of Hat until then. The young narrator is not simply wide-eyed in his uncritical acceptance of Hat and the others but it is clear that he absorbs their code until he is forced to a decision and chooses to leave for London. He reveals that Hat is a petty criminal, often in trouble with the law, but he had preferred until now to think of him differently. He introduces the portrait, 'Hat loved to make a mystery of the smallest things', and expresses his admiration: 'I never knew a man who enjoyed life as much as Hat did.' But the narrator is forced to face the facts about Hat, and, perhaps with some regret, he admits that the central incident breaks up 'the Miguel Street Club, and Hat himself was never the same afterwards'.[27] The incident involves a woman who appears in Hat's life one day, although until this point the narrator has concealed any information about Hat's sexual life, and now, in middle age, Hat appears rather desperate to keep the woman. When she leaves him for another man, Hat follows her and becomes so violent that he actually believes he has killed her. Although he has not indeed killed her, he is sentenced to four years in jail. 'Hat's homecoming fell a little flat. It wasn't only that we boys had grown older. Hat too had changed. Some of the brightness had left him.'[28] By now the narrator is old enough to think for himself, to look 'critically' at the life of the street. What he had interpreted as Hat's brightness, his enjoyment of life, his relaxed demeanour all day long, is now revealed to be akin to Bogart's boredom and languor; they are both desperately making their way through a haphazard life with few rewards or satisfactions. The narrator knows that the roles they all play are disguises for their sense of being trapped in poverty with few choices, nor are they eager to take on responsibilities or a more disciplined way of life.

But the narrator does not make explicit judgements. He remains sympathetic and rather elegiac in the face of the facts that are revealed. 'Hat' included an awareness of time passing and change, of wasted lives, of the necessity of choice if one wanted to have an individual life of more substance than that of the film-star imitations. In the final story, the narrator's own character becomes central, for in choosing to leave Trinidad, he turns aside from reproducing the life he has known. Yet the collection of stories retains much of the narrator's sense of wonder at how lives evolve and reveal themselves in small gestures, savouring the comic and sometimes eccentric textures of the lives on the street. This is an inescapable part of what the narrator has absorbed, and from his more mature, retrospective distance, he curtails the critical way of understanding what he observes and records. On that day in 1955, it was this discovery of a narrative voice that allowed the characters their own autonomy, their freedom as dramatic presences to reveal themselves and, in doing so, to reveal the reality of their communal culture.

Miguel Street is not only a representation of Luis Street, Port of Spain, however, at a particular moment in the 1940s, or of a colonial society close to a condition of stasis and hopelessness; it is also an exemplifica-tion of a way of telling a story that included Naipaul's own feelings covertly so that the style reflected the reality he had known. It is revealed that the narrator is situated outside Trinidad, and so he is recreating the street from memory, and from a distance, yet the method is to get as close as possible to the voices of the street and to a young person's innocent discovery of them. Naipaul is inventing the role of writer, outside his native culture in which there was not yet such a role, and he is conscious that it is a new role almost without models. Naipaul has said that in his adolescence the cinema was as powerful a presence as literature in his life, and so the roles Bogart and Hat took from the cinema interest him, but in his own case inventing the role of writer and dramatizing it became a preoccupation throughout his career. 'Prologue to an Autobiography' tells how the role was invented suc-cessfully for the first time.

'Prologue' is shaped in part by the story of what happened in the BBC room but more so by explorations of the lives of the two people who were critical to this beginning—the man whom the street had nick-named Bogart and Naipaul's father. The young man whom Hat tries to rouse each morning lived briefly in a room behind the house Naipaul's immediate family shared with many other members of his mother's family. 'Hat', Naipaul explains,

wasn't Negro or mulatto. But we thought of him as half way there. He was a Port of Spain Indian. The Port of Spain Indians—there were pockets of them—had no country roots, were individuals, hardly a community, and were separate from us for an additional reason: many of them were Madrassis, descendants of South India, not Hindu-speaking, and not people of caste. We didn't see in them any of our own formalities or restrictions.[29]

But Bogart was different: connected to another branch of Naipaul's mother's family, he had drifted into temporary residence in the city and, attempting to free himself from the 'restrictions' of the traditional and insulated Hindu community, had accepted a kind of membership in the 'world of the street'. Over the years, Naipaul became fascinated by the mystery of Bogart, and in the 1970s he traced him to Venezuela and visited him there. But in choosing to investigate in more depth the character of this migrant, the author of 'Prologue' recognizes implicitly that he had found in him a certain kinship and in the street population a condition that he would experience himself and needed to understand.

The role of Bogart that this man had played on the street was only a small part of how he set about inventing a free life for himself, and Naipaul's father was also such a person: a self-educated countryman who had migrated to the city and become a journalist. He too wished to be free of the 'restrictions' of the extended Hindu family, and in English literature he found another kind of identity: he aspired to be a writer published in London and to capture in fiction some essential qualities of his displaced Indian community and its cultural affiliations with the traditions of the subcontinent. He began to write stories, and when Naipaul was about ten, a small collection was published in Trinidad, *Gurudeva and Other Indian Tales*. 'I was involved in the slow making of ['Gurudeva'] from the beginning to the end', Naipaul reports.

Every new bit was read out to me, every little variation; and I read every new typescript my father made as the story grew. It was the greatest imaginative experience of my childhood.... And then somehow, without any discussion that I remember, it seemed to be settled, in my mind as well as my father's, that I was to be a writer.[30]

The narrative strand in 'Prologue', which traces Naipaul's first inheritance from his father, explores ambition and anxiety, failure, breakdown and modest success, all this in the face of a deep ambivalence of attitude. 'The ambition to be a writer was given to me by my father', he writes, but he goes on to conclude: 'it was that fear, a panic about failing to be what I should be, rather than simple ambition, that was with me when I came down from Oxford in 1954.'[31] When he left Trinidad in 1950 to take up a scholarship at Oxford, Naipaul's plan was to write novels rather than to be a scholar, and in leaving the island, he also wished to set a distance between himself and the material his father had written about, for his goal was to be a writer in the context of London literary life and to discover his subjects there.

In the alienated years he spent at Oxford, however, during which he remained in very close contact by letter with his father until the latter's early death in 1953, Naipaul gradually began to consider how his Caribbean background provided him with the material he might write about, first for the BBC programme 'Caribbean Voices', on which some of his father's new work was also broadcast.

One day, deep in my almost fixed depression, I began to see what my material might be: the city street from whose mixed life we had held aloof, and the country life before that, with the ways and manners of a remembered India. It seemed easy and obvious when it had been found, but it had taken me four years to see it.... To get started as a writer, I had had to go back to the beginning, and pick my way back—forgetting Oxford and London—to those early literary experiences.[32]

Patrick French writes that aspects of the characters in the stories reminded Naipaul's family and others of people they had known in the Port of Spain neighbourhood, but for all its local colour, dialect, and 'artful simplicity', French writes, it is 'an ambitious and remarkable book'. 'Pa's legacy', French continues, 'the critical success of Sam Selvon [the Trinidadian novelist], the high standards set by Henry Swanzy and the encouragement and example of other writers on "Caribbean Voices" convinced Vidia that good literature could be written about his own country.'[33] Turning away from the anxious ambition he had to write with an authority won in Oxford—something his father never had an opportunity to gain—Naipaul found a confidence in a certain kind of identification with his father's work and the knowledge of Trinidadian life that was embedded in it.

Naipaul mentions a number of times that knowledge came to him as he wrote *Miguel Street*, and in part that knowledge, like the voice in which it is articulated, was derived from his father's life. In his newspaper work, Seepersad Naipaul had written of 'village feuds, family vendettas, murders, bitter election battles', the social manifestations of a deeper disquiet and psychic disorder. As a young person, he had experienced great cruelty and poverty, and 'the network of Hindu reverences' in the family scarcely sustained him. But in his stories, he had found a style that mixed romance with fairytale and traditional lore: 'These stories celebrated Indian village life', Naipaul writes in 'Prologue',

and the Hindu rituals that gave grace and completeness to that life. They also celebrated elemental things, the order of the working day, the labour of the rice-fields, the lighting of the cooking fire in the half-walled gallery of a thatched hut, the preparation and eating of food.... [But the longest story] added cruelty, and comedy that made the cruelty just bearable. It was my private epic.[34]

The father's distress and frustration at the instability and disorder, the 'cheated hopes' and 'tormented time' that characterized his own life, seemed to be alleviated only by a calm he experienced while writing. And reading: 'His idea of the writer—as a person triumphant and detached—was a private composite of O. Henry, Warwick Deeping, Marie Corelli [bestselling writers of the early decades of the century], Charles Dickens, Somerset Maugham, and J. R. Ackerley (of *Hindoo Holiday*).'[35] It was, Naipaul writes, 'a fantasy of nobility' his father passed on to him, but until that day in the freelance room, he had not discovered how to draw on that inheritance.

In that BBC room, his father's work was respected, and it was there too that 'Bogart' had its first readers. They were wholeheartedly in favour of the new work. Three colleagues on 'Caribbean Voices' read it, and encouraged him to keep writing. They and Naipaul himself worked inside a very supportive milieu, created over some years for the programme and Caribbean writing generally by the producer Henry Swanzy. Like Diana Athill, the Irish-born Swanzy searched for an authentic literature from other places outside the English mainstream, not romantic or exotic or pandering in any way to imperial perspectives. He had praised the work of Seepersad Naipaul and welcomed the young Oxford graduate into the programme in three different roles: reader, writer, and presenter. For a decade already, Swanzy had sought out and broadcast poets and novelists from the Caribbean, and while many of his contributors had migrated to London, he also had an agent based in Jamaica who forwarded new work to him. To a degree, the local voices heard on the programme must have reassured

Naipaul that a literary version of them was indeed the appropriate voice he needed for his authentic work.[36] And so Bogart and the men on the street are brought to life largely through their dialect conversations but additionally by the voice of the narrator of the stories. It may even be that writing stories for radio broadcast rather than to be read, and then, in the early months of 1955, presenting the programme in Swanzy's absence, and the presence of so many Caribbean writers as friends and colleagues at this time all contributed to the oral qualities of the plain literary voice that Naipaul invented.

∾

Naipaul's method in *Miguel Street* is to preserve much of the 'innocence' of an earlier stage of his life, even though he and his narrator are writing from an outside and distant place.

> It was a 'flat' view of the street: in what I had written I went right up close to it, as close as I had been as a child, shutting out what lay outside. I knew even then that there were other ways of looking; that if, so to speak, I took a step or two or three back and saw more of the setting, it would require another kind of writing.[37]

In a sense, he was released in the writing from the complications and explanations he would return to later, after the four works of Trinidad fiction, when he wrote *The Middle Passage* and began to travel to other Caribbean islands and to India. In contrast to the immediacy of the fiction, his intention then was to gain an intellectual understanding of the migration of his ancestors from India as indentured servants on sugar plantations, of their cultural displacement and settling, and to add insights based on empirical historical research about the earlier colonial settlements of the island.

This work would become the next phase of his career, yet it is striking that even in that non-fiction book, in which Naiapul writes in a strong and opinionated authorial voice of impressions gathered during his stay in Trinidad in 1961, the long essay begins:

> As soon as the *Francisco Bobadillo* had touched the quay, ship's side against rubber bumpers, I began to feel all my old fear of Trinidad. I did not want to stay. I had left the security of the ship and had no assurance that I would ever leave the island again.... The threat of failure, the need to escape: this was the prompting of the society I knew.[38]

The essay develops into a caustic examination of a chaotic colonial society of many races and traditions, a failed society that lacks self-confidence

or purpose and looks elsewhere for guidelines on identity and presentation of self. This essay and the long historical account in *The Loss
of El Dorado* later in the 1960s are driven by a kind of anguish that was
submerged in *Miguel Street*. The fictions set in Trinidad, or in the
Caribbean island of Isabella in *The Mimic Men*, are actually continuous
in their feelings of fear, the need for self-dramatization, and the loss of
self in such a society. Even though Naipaul will later refer to the 'der-
eliction and despair' his father knew personally, 'a vision of disorder
and destitution, of which he discovered himself to be a part', and then
praise his father's calm and comic tone, he knows that it was 'a way of
concealing personal pain'.[39]

Diana Athill has written a shrewd memoir of the Naipaul she knew at
this time in which she touches on his 'fear and dislike of Trinidad', 'the
nervous defiance of disrespect', and 'his need to protect his pride' which
marked his presentation of self: 'I had no conception of how someone
who feels he doesn't belong to his "home" and cannot belong anywhere
else is forced to exist only in himself.'[40] She also remarks on 'the authority
of his account of Mr Biswas's nervous collapse', assuming it drew on his
father's state and not realizing until later that 'its painful vividness' had an
autobiographical source.[41] It is clear that Naipaul's sympathetic identification with the pain and entrapment that led to his father's breakdown,
and which he writes of so movingly in 'Prologue', lie underneath his own
fear and 'the need to escape'. They also underlie and are concealed by the
narrative voice he found for *Miguel Street*, for this is the more complete
inheritance he received from his father as man and writer.

The fictional method Naipaul associates with a child's perspective,
without judgement or explanation, is a deliberate departure from
omniscience and recalls the impersonal method of modernist writers.
He allows himself to hint at this in two fictionalized versions. In *A Way
in the World*, he writes about 'Foster Morris's' advice to him to abandon
the novel he had just completed and to read:

He wanted me to read certain writers—Chekhov, Hemingway and his
beloved Graham Greene—and he wanted me to pay attention to the way they
wrote. He wanted me to think more about writing. And he was right. . . . I had
thought of it as something that would come naturally to me. I hadn't thought
of it as something I would have to learn about and try to understand.[42]

It may well be that the 'spontaneous' writing of 'Bogart' was not so spontaneous, after all, but was actually a response to this advice. Two further

comments—'I set my narrator at the level of the street. I found an immense freedom in this touch of fiction'—suggest that the placing of the narrative perspective did not come 'naturally' but was actually a liberation from the burden of being a more detached or omniscient narrator.

There is another hint of this in the novel *Half a Life*. When Willie Chandran arrives in London and writes stories of India, he receives advice from an Englishman, Roger: 'Life doesn't have a neat beginning and a tidy end. Life is always going on. You should begin in the middle and end in the middle, and it should be all there.'[43] Roger has practical advice: 'Have you read Hemingway? You should read the early stories. There's one called "The Killers".' Willie takes this advice, reads 'The Killers', and reworks his story:

The story, as he thought of it, became almost all dialogue. Everything was to be contained in the dialogue. The setting and the people weren't to be explained. That undid a lot of the difficulty. He had only to begin, the story rewrote itself, and though in one way it was now very far from Willie, it was also much more full of his feeling.[44]

What Willie Chandran learned about an impersonal, plain style as a powerful method for intensified feeling surely derives from what the novelist learned in 1955 and explained earlier in 'Prologue' in almost exactly similar terms, without reference to Hemingway's work.

In Naipaul's critical writing, modernist writers are rarely mentioned, however, and apart from these very pertinent references to Hemingway in a novel, the American writer is dismissed elsewhere. But if the method of the early stories of Hemingway actually lies behind *Miguel Street*, there is surely another presence behind Hemingway's stories, never mentioned by Naipaul: Joyce's *Dubliners*. While Graham Greene, Evelyn Waugh, and Aldous Huxley were among the most prominent writers of the mid-century in Britain, a figure such as Joyce, like Hemingway, writing in another idiom and deliberately situating himself in literary traditions outside the Empire, had something different to offer Naipaul. Patrick French does not mention Hemingway or Joyce in his biography, and only one critic appears to have recognized their importance for Naipaul at this pivotal time. '[The stories of *Miguel Street*] are his *Dubliners*', Bruce King writes, 'and *A Portrait of the Artist as a Young Man*. They show why it was necessary to leave and to remain away from home.'[45]

Eschewing the omniscient narrator and the realism of nineteenth-century English fiction, many of Joyce's stories are set on the streets of Dublin, using narrators who are closely identified with the voices of the protagonists and their world. In particular, the opening stories enact a child's awareness of the mysteries of adult life, and especially of a kind of psychic paralysis that is traced to cultural and economic stagnation in Irish society. The first story, 'The Sisters', even begins with the child protagonist recognizing that certain words seem to be a secret key to the character of the priest who is dying. It is surely not fortuitous that Hat's question to Bogart, 'What happening there?', instantly draws attention to the fact that nothing of significance is happening, or will happen, for Naipaul's street life of Port of Spain resembles that of Joyce's Dublin in stories like 'Two Gallants', 'Counterparts', or 'The Boarding House'. *Miguel Street* presents a Caribbean version of Joycean 'paralysis'. Naipaul's characters, like Joyce's, are largely trapped by poverty and inertia, by varieties of male escapism and violence, but, most of all, it is Joyce's unusual tone of sympathy and detachment that links his stories to 'Bogart' and the others. 'I explained nothing', Naipaul has said. 'I stayed at ground level, so to speak. I presented people only as they appeared on the street.'[46] The idea of revealing the reality of a place or community through understated epiphanies and brief stories is not uniquely Joycean, but rather than considering Steinbeck's *Cannery Row* or Sherwood Anderson's *Winesburg, Ohio*, or, perhaps, Dickens's *Sketches by Boz*, the Joycean model is surely the most likely influence. Reinforcing this model, Bruce King remarks 'the stories are astringent in their ironies'.[47]

Although Naipaul has never written about Joyce, he shows an early awareness of his importance. In New York, on his way to London in 1950, he reported to his sister that he had noted books by Joyce and Hemingway in a bookstore, although he did not buy them, and in August 1953, he wrote to his father that he will send him *Dubliners*, which he has clearly read with some care. 'James Joyce', he tells his father, 'wrote that story "Clay" in the Everyman selection. The one you liked so much that you read it to me'. It is surely remarkable that in his reading of *Dubliners* in 1953, this memory of his father's voice is associated with Joyce.[48] It may have been the friendship with Henry Swanzy that brought Naipaul's attention back to Joyce in 1953, but even without the Irishman's presence, Joyce was widely known as a writer who had left his homeland and in his exile had drawn on very precise memories to create great literature. In general, Naipaul has underplayed his interest in European classic literature, or been critical of figures like Flaubert or Conrad, but this may be because he wishes to situate his own work outside such European traditions. There is one crucial, early illustration, however, of Naipaul self-consciously situating himself in a modernist context. In the chapter on Trinidad in *The Middle Passage*, he includes an epigraph from Thomas Mann that reads in part: 'they were now unanchored souls, wavering in spirit and without a secure doctrine. They had forgotten much; they had half-assimilated some new thoughts; and because they lacked real orientation, they did not trust their own feelings.'[49] Naipaul is already characterizing himself as a migrant writer, like so many moderns, but there may be an 'anxiety of influence' at play in his bid for a unique voice without influences. It is tempting to see the posture of Stephen Dedalus as he moves away into a state of 'silence, exile and cunning' as something that might have appealed to young Naipaul. The artist in exile is certainly a self-image that remained central to Naipaul's sense of himself all through his career, and indeed his constant return to consider his own 'way of see-ing' situates him as author/artist in a modernist context that includes Joyce as well as Proust.[50]

While the memories from years before and his father's stories are clearly important, it appears that the decision to choose a particular nar-rative method, drawing on his reading of Joyce and Hemingway, is what really allowed Naipaul to write in a new and liberating way. 'The aim has always been to fill out my world picture', he said in the Nobel address, 'and the purpose comes from my childhood: to make me more at ease with myself'.[51] In grounding *Miguel Street* in something he may think of as a child's 'perfect view', he allows the voices of the characters them-selves to establish the 'centre' of the place and does not pass overt judge-ment on them. They are dramatized, but the narrator is not, until the end, and so the understanding of his fear and of the need to leave Trinidad remain implicit and impersonal, and yet they govern the vision and method of the stories. These stories, like *Dubliners*, constitute a chap-ter in the 'moral history' of the writer's native place, from which he has deliberately separated himself, and yet he must recover it and clarify for himself the nature of the unease he irrevocably absorbed there.

∼

While *Miguel Street* and the three novels written immediately after-wards grow out of an immersion in memories of his earliest years, Naipaul's way of investigating his years of apprenticeship serves him in the writing of autobiographical narratives that actually distance him from the role of 'Caribbean' writer. They reflect his later development and its many new beginnings. 'Knowledge came to me rapidly during the writing', he sums up in *The Enigma of Arrival*,

and with that knowledge, that acknowledgement of myself (so hard before it was done, so very easy and obvious afterwards), my curiosity grew fast. I did other work; and in this concrete way, out of work that came easily to me because it was so close to me, I defined myself, and saw that my subject was not my sensibility, my inward development, but the worlds I contained within myself, the worlds I lived in.[52]

The BBC room with its community of Caribbean writers, and, indeed, Naipaul's own experience of living close to poverty and nervous breakdown in London, reflected the reality of migration and so connected deeply with what the child had observed of Bogart and the rough 'world of the street'. That local place connected with a larger experience of the world: 'Out of a great mental fog there had come to me the idea of the street. And all at once, within a matter of days, material and tone of voice and writing skill had locked together and begun to develop together.'[53] Only some years later will Naipaul consciously recognize that this moment gave him a temporary poise and confidence that he would draw on to explore many parts of the world and his own self through a long career.

In 'Reading and Writing', he sums up the early novels and stories: 'Every book was a stage in a process of finding out; it couldn't be repeated. My material—my past, separated from me by place as well— was fixed and, like childhood itself, complete; it couldn't be added to. This way of writing consumed it. Within five years I had come to an end.'[54] But if he had exhausted the material, and he needed, as he has said, to broaden his perspective on the colonial condition through travelling and research, his way of seeing the material in the first stories stayed with him. 'As my world widened, beyond the immediate personal circumstances that bred fiction, and as my comprehension widened, the literary forms I practised flowed together and supported one another.'[55] He is referring to travel writing and autobiography and the way in which a method of writing fiction was enlarged through his learning how to write in these genres. But it is striking how what he refers to as 'narrative' grows in the writing out of the materials that have presented themselves. In other words, as in *Miguel Street*, when he writes of India or the Caribbean, he stays close to 'ground level'; he observes contexts, seizes on images, but primarily his focus is on individuals who, in presenting themselves to him, allow him to see not simply how they make sense of their own lives but how their culture and their place offer them ways of thinking and behaving. His reading of cultures and communities is a kind of anthropology based on a very close dramatization of individuals, a fiction-writer's method or 'way of seeing'. Writing about his travels in India, Naipaul remarks, 'what was most important about a travel book were the people the writer travelled among. The people had to define themselves.'[56]

Apart from the early travel books, *The Middle Passage* and *An Area of Darkness*, the next stage of his development is marked by the novel *The Mimic Men*. It is autobiographical in form, or, rather, as in *The Enigma of Arrival* and *A Way in the World*, and, indeed, 'Prologue', it presents a life through the process of searching to find a way of telling the story. It is his first work of fiction in which a character of Caribbean background is presented living in London. In this narrative investigation of the life of Ralph Singh, there are many flashbacks to earlier stages of his life in London and especially in Isabella, a Caribbean island where he became for a time a man of wealth and power until his government was overthrown and he was exiled. The voice of the writer in the present telling of this life is central to the novel, however, and, significantly, in spite of exile and impoverishment, he concludes: 'writing, for all its distortion, clarifies, and even becomes a process of life.'[57] This is a fiction about how he becomes a writer, not a successful one, or one with a new social role, but one who sees the truth of his experience, and so, once again, this time on a higher social and economic class, Naipaul investigates the character of a 'mimic', a Bogartian character, a colonial who becomes a migrant and a writer.

In the Nobel address, he explains: 'This new fiction was about colonial shame and fantasy, a book, in fact, about how the powerless lie about themselves, and lie to themselves, since it is their only resource.'[58] He continues in terms that recall even more directly his intuitive preoccupation with the 'Club' of men in *Miguel Street* ten years earlier: 'It was about colonial men mimicking the condition of manhood, men who had grown to distrust everything about themselves.' And he insists that he had no theory of 'colonial schizophrenia' guiding him when he wrote: 'The book was done intuitively and out of close observation.'[59] In a sense, it is a novel about someone like the narrator of *Miguel Street*, who went away and understood so much, but not enough, and so abused his freedom until, disgraced, he had to find a new kind of freedom without power or position. *The Mimic Men* may be seen as the first in a series that includes *In a Free State* and *The Bend in the River*, fictions set in wider worlds and exploring the conditions of displacement, migration, or homelessness, all relying on a powerful narrative voice or voices to establish a sense of self.

'I am the sum of my books', Naipaul insists. 'Each book, intuitively sensed and, in the case of fiction, intuitively worked out, stands on what has gone before.'[60] He is speaking on the Nobel occasion in 1999, but this understanding of how his career is founded on his trust in intuition goes back not only to 'Prologue to an Autobiography' but to the actual writing of *Miguel Street*. The method he found for 'narrative', for fusing observation and autobiography, liberated him in the writing from fear and failure. After he had come to believe that he had succeeded as a professional writer, and had escaped much of the 'panic and the fear of the abyss', he declared in 1985:

I write now out of something like joy—joy at having found a subject, a theme, something new (yet always obvious, after the discovery) to work on. A new piece of writing is perhaps the only thing that truly engages my mind. It is still wonderful to me when a piece of writing catches fire. I live completely then.[61]

This echoes the experience in the BBC room in 1955 when for the first time that kind of intense focus and energy came to him as a liberation from his inherited limitations, a mastery of powerlessness: 'the book was written out of the joy of that discovery.'[62]

2

Alice Munro's *Dance of the Happy Shades*

The personal voice

Lives of Girls and Women was Alice Munro's first collection of stories to be published internationally, although for twenty years her work had been known in Canada.[1] This apparently autobiographical fiction of Del Jordan's childhood and adolescence in 'Jubilee', Munro's fictional version of her first home in rural and small-town Ontario, is 'part way between a novel and a series of long stories', actually eight linked stories with this common setting and a first-person narrator.[2] Canadian readers had already glimpsed this imaginative territory, recollected and recreated from more than two thousand miles away in Vancouver and Victoria. An earlier collection, *Dance of the Happy Shades* (1968), included stories of the 1950s and 1960s, but in fact much of that time was spent, frustratingly, in a series of efforts to write a novel. The stories were written, as it seemed to Munro at the time, on the margin of her main ambition, and it was only when she abandoned the role of novelist (although salvaging many fragments for stories) that she recognized herself as a writer of poetic fiction. 'I learned that I was never going to write a real novel because I could not think that way',[3] she has said, prompting many interviewers to enquire what her 'way' of thinking is, but Munro insists that her method is intuitive and that she is not capable of analysing her own fiction or how it is produced. The recognition that she had to write 'personal' fiction—and in her view this is distinct from autobiographical fiction—came gradually, and is inseparable from the artistic decision to create Jubilee, to find the appropriate style to embody the reality of that place and what she had

learned there. This emerging clarification may be seen in stages, especially in three stories, 'The Peace of Utrecht', written in 1959, and
'Walker Brothers Cowboy' and 'Images', both written in late 1967, and
these stories are the foundation for the integrated fictions of *Lives of
Girls and Women* and for much of her later work.[4]

Munro has often spoken of the harsh economic and physical circumstances in which she was raised near Wingham, Ontario in the
1930s and 1940s. She has also shown a keen interest in how individuals'
lives are shaped by particular historical periods: the frontier settlements
of her ancestors in late nineteenth-century Ontario, the Depression
and the war years of her parents and their generation, the 1960s with
the sexual and other kinds of liberations that it fostered, and, in later
life, the eighteenth-century community in Scotland from which the
earliest immigrants in her family came and settled in North America.
Her keen observation of historical change and how individuals are
confined and liberated in their daily lives might have made her a realistic novelist, perhaps even a writer of naturalist fiction, but she was not
drawn to the nineteenth-century novel as a model for her fictional
images of historically conditioned lives. She acknowledges the reality
of physical and economic conditions, but insists that she is not a writer
of 'ideas' about them, or indeed about political or philosophical matters. As a writer, she thinks of storytelling as an experiment to discover
the vision in the story that may come as close as possible to the felt
reality of the life situation she has been compelled to investigate.

From adolescent years, Munro wrote poems—she has spoken of her
excitement in discovering Tennyson, for instance—and her archived
papers include her earliest imitations of Tennyson and other unpub-
lished poems from this time and much later.[5] The importance of this
is, I believe, that she has always been a writer for whom the emotion
in her prose is charged by images of place or setting rather than by
dramatic episodes, plot, or character. In fact, she remarked on the 'den-
sity about place that transcends the story completely'.[6] This suggests
that it is not simply accuracy of observation of Jubilee for sociological
or historical record that interests her but for the psychological reality
of things, the 'furniture' of her 'houses', as she puts it. Descriptive
details of clothing, of work, of domestic objects, of animals and landscape, of town streets, and then of the rhythms of voice, both conver-
sational voices and narrative voice, convey intense poetic resonances
and the depth of lived experience.

It is this depth of feeling that interests her, not so much the photograph as the inner states that are captured in a characteristic moment or gesture, and Munro has actually spoken of her attraction to the work of certain photographers and painters. 'I'm very interested in photography', she remarked, 'but photographs are too explicit to relate to stories'.[7] She frequently speaks of 'vision' as well as visualization, and in the opening story of *Lives*, a kind of prologue that introduces the notion of Del's artistic awakening, the narrator remarks of a storytelling neighbour, 'all this seemed to grow up around us created by his monotonous, meticulously remembering voice, and we could see it.... It was his triumph ... to make us see.'[8] The Epilogue to the collection is entitled 'The Photographer', and in it the adult Del looks back to an adolescent phase when she wanted to write a novel about her home town of Jubilee. The photographer is a figure who comes to the town and frightens people by the truth he reveals in his photographs. Munro's initial title for *Lives of Girls and Women* was 'Real Life', and as her career progressed, artlessness, a fidelity to the feeling of 'life itself' unconstrained by 'fictionalizing', became her measure of success.

Although Munro prides herself on how truthfully she observes and grounds her work in the realities of an existing world, she also knows that styles of indirection and displacement in storytelling interest her and, in particular, the pressures of interpretation and subjective beliefs and visions. Many of her narrators confide to being self-conscious about the process of story-making based on selective observation, and Munro frequently blurs the distinction between her authorial presence and her narrative voice. In a family story, 'Winter Wind', the narrator asks, 'how am I to know what I claim to know? ... Yet I have not invented it, I really believe it. Without any proof I believe it, and so I must believe that we get messages another way, that we have connections that cannot be investigated, but have to be relied on.'[9] She has confessed to often having difficulties knowing whether a story works best with a first-person or a third-person narrator, and many stories have been written both ways; knowing that her goal is to capture the greatest depth of feeling, Munro has remarked that sometimes personal material is not best told by a first-person narrator.[10] Uncertainty about narrative voice appears to mirror uncertainty about authorial voice also, or, indeed, fidelity to the conflicted and unresolved significance of felt experience. The doubts of her narrators reflect her own questioning of the relationship between life and art and their separate kinds of reality. This tension between a shaping imagination and revealed patterns in life, on the one hand, and the uncontrollable and unpredictable nature of life's evolution, on the other, is constant.

The challenge of finding narrative voices, especially once she accepted that her primary material was personal, became central. 'If I had been making a proper story out of this', the narrator confides in 'The Ottawa Valley', 'I would have ended it, I think, with my mother not answering and going ahead of me across the pasture. That would have done. I didn't stop there, I suppose, because I wanted to find out more, remember more. I wanted to bring back all I could.'[11] Narrator and author are indistinguishable in this story in *Something I Have Been Meaning to Tell You*. Her first solution to this difficulty of voice was to recognize that her style must be an incorporation of voices that are rooted in the experience she had known best in her place of origin. She discovered that she must allow those felt voices to speak, especially by creating an authorial/narrative voice that merged her childhood and adult sensibilities.

In a sense, then, it may be said that Alice Munro's vision and art are regional and rooted in one place. Although she once confessed to feeling that she had used up all her childhood material, and many later stories do move into urban settings and multi-generational timeframes, throughout her career and even in her final collection she returns to the childhood and familial material of her early experience in Huron County, Ontario. The memoir and family history stories—written occasionally over thirty years and collected in *The View from Castle Rock*, and the closing section of *Dear Life*, her final collection of stories— reaffirm that her lasting identity as a writer is inextricable from that early stage when she discovered a voice for her country place, for her mother and father, and for herself as narrator of the 'real life' she found there. Articulating the foundational vision of 'real life' in those early circumstances liberated her into ways of articulating other lives shaped by other circumstances and time periods. What she discovered in finding her own first identity as an artist remained to inform all later stages of her career.

~

'There are few pleasures in writing to equal that of creating your town', Alice Munro wrote in 1974, 'exploring the pattern of it, feeling all those lives, and streets, and hidden rooms and histories, coming to light, seeing all the ceremonies and attitudes and memories in your power'.[12] She was writing while she was still inventing stories of Jubilee, but, in fact, she grew up outside the town of Wingham, on a small farm next to swamps and bush, and came to know it well only during her later school years. While the town of Jubilee is coloured by adolescent experiences and perceptions, she had already written stories of the earlier world of the small farm, which her parents had bought when they married in 1927. In this miniature world of family, farm and rough countryside, she imagined a whole enriched world, darkened from a distance by reflection. In fact she was 'alienated' from this world and settled far away from it: 'I grew up in a rural community, a very traditional community ... but I always realized that I had a different view of the world, and one that would bring me into great trouble and ridicule if it were exposed.'[13] Its creation was a complex act of recovery rather than simply recollection or recording, and this is especially true of her exploration of her relationships with her mother and father. They provided her with the material for a whole vision of life and art, and so her impoverished and alienated upbringing is where her imagination first grew and then began to find its fictional medium after more than a decade of apprenticeship in story-writing.

Alice Laidlaw was born in 1931 in south-western Ontario, perhaps one hundred miles west of Toronto and quite close to Lake Huron. She was the eldest of three children. Her nineteenth-century ancestors were of Scottish Presbyterian and Irish Anglican backgrounds, hard-working farmers who had survived with various degrees of self-sufficiency in isolated and introverted cultural circumstances. Her mother, Anne Chamney, qualified as an elementary teacher but had ambitions to move into a more secure and middle-class way of life. In marrying Robert Laidlaw and investing her savings from her years of teaching in a fox fur business, her aspirations to leave the condition of mere survival behind led the family to have more security than many during the Depression. Their business collapsed, however, in the war years, and Robert Laidlaw found manual work at the foundry in Wingham before beginning a new business as a turkey farmer. 'Working for a Living', a memoir Munro wrote after his death, honours her father for his grace in impoverished circumstances, and she has elsewhere affirmed that he was a man of significant talent, a self-educated reader who at the end of his life wrote a novel.[14]

Anne Chamney struggled to preserve a lady-like poise in circumstances she found demeaning, in a house without electricity, running water, or toilet, situated beyond the edge of town and at the end of an unpaved stretch of road with uneducated neighbours surviving close to destitution. Their small fox farm adjoined wild countryside, where many eccentric trappers and lawless characters lived haphazard lives. The farmwork involved the raising of great numbers of foxes in cages at a distance from the house, the killing of old horses for meat for the foxes, and then, when the foxes were killed, the house became the site of the removal of the skins and the preparation of the fur for sale. This physical and visceral reality of the domestic and work environment was not much to Anne Chamney's taste,[15] but Munro's imagination engaged indelibly with her father's world and his life beyond her mother's influence. Something else, even more immediately physical, marked her adolescent experience of her mother—serious and debilitating illness. Signs of what would later be diagnosed as Parkinson's disease began to appear when Munro was twelve, and her mother slipped more and more into extreme forms of incapacitation. Her dependence on her elder daughter for basic housekeeping was accompanied by the even more humiliating dependence on her to interpret her increasingly laboured efforts to speak.

The stories reveal that all these circumstances left intense and vivid recollections and material for reflection that enriched Munro's fiction for decades, but already she was not merely an observer. In an impulse to invent separate imagined worlds, she had begun to make up stories and then to write poems and stories and to plan a novel. Reading was encouraged in her home, and from early years she had begun to find in classic novels, such as *Wuthering Heights*, and Lucy Maud Montgomery's *Emily of New Moon*, places that she could enter pleasurably and experience a heightened imaginative state. A very talented high school student, she won a scholarship to university. She studied Journalism and English for two years at the University of Western Ontario, but spent most of her time on stories, some of which were published in a university journal, and by age twenty she had started to send them to the *New Yorker*. Although she failed to have any accepted there through the 1950s, she had already caught the attention of Robert Weaver, who regularly accepted stories for broadcast on the Canadian Broadcasting Corporation and also in his literary magazine, *Tamarack Review*. Equally significant as this first success during her university years was the fact that she met Jim Munro, a fellow student who supported her writing. She married him in late 1951 and moved to Vancouver, where he had found a job and where she quickly became a suburban mother and homemaker. She continued to write, and to earn a respectable income from magazine publication, but the move to Vancouver at age twenty left her in an urban setting far from her home and family. In short, she began an entirely new life there, and in the many years before her mother's death in early 1959, she rarely returned to visit her parents, nor did she return to Ontario for her mother's funeral.

These biographical details of youthful alienation and deliberate uprooting do not in themselves explain much of how her imagination engaged with the material of her original place and led to the creation eventually of an art that won her world-wide recognition, yet this remark is suggestive of the impact of her migration: 'You do become a different person in a lot of superficial ways to make yourself acceptable in the world away from home. You were apt to feel perhaps a bit of a phony, I suppose, when you went back home. Who are you then? Which person? How do you talk?...I find this very interesting and compli-cated.'[16] In the first decade, she accepted material wherever she found it and wrote many stories of suburban life in Vancouver, as well as some arising from recollections of her corner of Ontario. In later decades, she returned to accepting material from many sources, but in a crucial period, between the summer of 1959, when she wrote 'The Peace of Utrecht', and 1967 when she quickly wrote three stories to 'fill out' the collection a Toronto publisher had decided to publish in 1968, a trans-formation happened. She had continued to struggle with a novel through the 1960s, and wrote only a handful of stories, but it was follow-ing the stories of 1967, and the appearance of *Dance of the Happy Shades*, that she came to the decision to abandon the novel and reassess how to use the accumulating material of childhood and adolescence in Jubilee. The kind of refocusing on her art that can be identified in the stories of 1967 led on directly to *Lives of Girls and Women* and then to much of the work included in the next two collections in the 1970s, *Something I've Been Meaning to Tell You* and *Who Do You Think You Are?*[17] The childhood world she had fled, and then the small town of her youth, both proved to be the foundational material of her self-definition as an artist.

Her reading of fiction set in local places by celebrated authors encouraged her in this decision, but Munro also remained uncertain of this old-fashioned adherence to a vanishing rural world. 'I think that the kind of writing I do is almost anachronistic, because it's so rooted in one place, and most people, even of my age, do not have a place like this any more, and it's something that may not have meaning very much longer. I mean this kind of writing.'[18] Yet Munro felt compelled to create a vanishing world in all its concreteness in a kind of 'super realism', using a technique that she believed was 'very traditional, very conventional', and confesses to feeling that a comparison might be made with the paintings of Edward Hopper or Andrew Wyeth.[19] 'It seems to me very important to be able to get at the exact tone or texture of how things are. I can't really claim that it is linked to any kind of religious feeling about the world, and yet that might come close to describing it.'[20] She does not offer the stories of James Joyce as a point of comparison, but this remark surely conceals Joyce's idea of the epiphany as the revelation of the reality of his local place, the city of Dublin.[21] Like Joyce, and later writers whose work Munro admired, her kind of super realism allies her with modernism, and what she self-deprecatingly calls 'conventional' is in fact the foundation of a body of work in the late twentieth century which is deeply personal, and experimental.

The most illuminating insight into Munro's early desire to become a writer and the kind of writer she wished to become are in the Afterword she wrote for *Emily of New Moon*, a novel she first read at nine or ten years of age and reread many times in following years.[22] The universal popularity of Montgomery's series of novels that grew out of *Anne of Green Gables* undoubtedly led Munro to the Emily series that followed, but this particular novel stands out because embedded in it Munro found the story of a girl's desire to become a writer. This brief Afterword affirms that from an early age Munro thought of herself as a writer and that this novel provided her with a confidence that her individual and private imaginings had validity as a way of being in the world, in spite of her desolating surroundings.

Munro recalls the simple pleasure of turning the pages, of being carried away into Emily's world, and in this sense it was 'a good book', but it was also disturbing and she found in it 'a demand for another kind of attention, the possibility of some new balance between myself and a book, between reader and writing'.[23] This disruption of the unselfconscious pleasure of following the narrative forced on Munro realities not easily accommodated in fantasy fiction: 'Emily is in trouble because she is an orphan, an outsider, and in fact because she is herself, because she is an outlaw at heart.' This sentence seems to reach past the experience of the child to the adult Munro herself. She continues to speak of 'a feeling of menace, and of complexity, of dark motives in family life', of disguised sexual tension, of 'something sadistic', 'something threatening', that Munro feels Montgomery was unable to really explore or control in her fiction. In recalling the unease her child-self felt, Munro is also detecting the limitations of Montgomery's art, and it is clear that Munro's adult self was drawn towards an exploration of just such tensions.

The novel was interesting for another reason, and they are hardly unrelated: 'the development of a child—a girl child, at that—into a writer ... [Emily] discovered writing as a way of surviving as herself in the world'.[24] One can see something of Munro's later work in the way she identifies the poetry and the prose in Emily's writing.

Poetry is her response to the things that give her 'the flash,' and 'the flash' itself is her moment of joy, of pure recognition, triggered by harmonies or oddities in the real world, or the bright edge on language, or a line of poetry already written. Prose is her way of dealing with people, and often with situations in which she is in fact powerless.

But her writing restores a sense of power to her. 'L. M. Montgomery makes us believe in "the flash," the moment of vision, the writing energy, the desperate commitment of a female child living on a farm in Prince Edward Island.' Clearly, in this autobiographical account, Munro allows us to see how the power of one book to change her sense of her own place was the foundation of her own desire to write. In addition to that sense of private imaginative empowerment, Munro explains why she returned to this book over and over in her teenage years: 'what was to matter most to me in books from then on was knowing more about that life than I'd been told, and more than I can tell'. Speaking of 'life spreading out behind the story—the book's life',[25] she introduces a sense of the rich mysteries in life that a talented writer can intuit and help readers to feel, without being explicit or expository in presenting that life. This is surely a major part of the 'real life' that adheres to the mundane and poetic details of everyday life on which all fiction is grounded for Alice Munro.

In speaking of 'the BIG influence from the time I was 12 to 14', *Wuthering Heights*, she remarks that 'all through my teens that was the kind of writing I was planning to do, and was working very hard on'.[26] While the Romanticism of the novel's vision may have appealed to her, something else in the world of *Wuthering Heights* was more fundamental—'the things that she [Catherine Earnshaw] did about the farm, the house, the fields'. Munro recalls the impact of specific details of landscape and place as if there were a foundational lesson here for her future writing of fiction: 'all that kind of detail which I think you have to do if you want to make up a novel of strong emotions that's credible'. She insists that she loved the novel for such details which allowed her to 'visualize everything—the way I was really living in that house'. Munro's discovery of an intense pleasure in entering isolated places in Prince Edward Island and Yorkshire is continuous with the mature writer working to make the reader visualize and enter fully into a specific place and experience 'strong emotions' there.

In her apprenticeship years, Munro was drawn to writers whose work captured something of her own vision of life and was written in styles that she tried to master. She has referred to writing 'exercises', some of which would catch the attention of magazine editors, her greatest effort in this regard being directed, unsuccessfully, at the *New Yorker*. She was an avid reader of the magazine in the 1950s and has mentioned trying to write in the style of Frank O'Connor, one of the successful writers the magazine published, but in the end she realized that his impersonal style did not suit her.[27] The magazine and two other publications, *New World Writing* and *Discovery*, gave her access to the work of the finest American short story writers, and she has mentioned, in particular, the Southern writers Carson McCullers, Flannery O'Connor, and Eudora Welty, although she read widely in contemporary fiction in the 1950s and 1960s, as well as classic writers such as Chekhov, Turgenev, and Henry James. But in talking about these writers, she is careful to distinguish between writers she admired and writers whom she believed may have influenced her, although on the matter of influence she insists that it was never conscious, and that her interest as a reader was the vision of the writer rather than his or her technique.[28]

Munro's reading of novels and short stories focused on striking and moving images taken from mundane circumstances, and this is at the heart of her appreciation of the writers she appears to have embraced most towards the end of the 1950s, James Agee and Eudora Welty. A brief contribution to a celebration of Welty's work exemplifies this.[29] Selecting from *The Golden Apples*, 'the first book of hers that I ever read and the one that turned out, finally, to be my favourite', Munro lists images or incidents 'that will probably stay with me forever', and her 'gratitude and amazed delight' may be measured by the length of the list and her affirmation that she could go on endlessly. Such enthusiasm is grounded in Welty's skill in thus creating a world, 'so true, as we say, to life', but more is involved since such observed details must be grounded in a felt vision of life: 'The story must be imagined so deeply and devoutly that everything in it seems to bloom of its own accord and to be connected, then, to our own lives which, suddenly, as we read, take on a hard beauty, a familiar strangeness, the importance of a dream which can't be disputed or explained.' In writing her appreciation of Welty's accomplishment, Munro recalls her own ambition as a writer; she had 'felt so unsure of my voice' and in 1959 and the following years she read Welty's work 'over and over' so that it became an inspiration for 'the kind of writing I most hoped to do'.[30]

Welty's invention of the Southern small town world of Morgana in the set of interconnected stories in *The Golden Apples* is surely a model for Munro's invention of Jubilee and for her return in the key stories of *Dance of the Happy Shades* to 'the familiar strangeness' of her first world in Huron County. In these stories may be found echoes of this appreciation and the ambition to write out of her own deepest self, and while she admired the rootedness of Welty's grasp of her place, Munro also found an element of her own vision that became central to these stories. 'I am overwhelmed', she wrote, 'with a terrible longing. Stabbed to the heart, as Miss Kate Rainey or perhaps Miss Perdita Mayo would say, by the changes, the losses in our lives. By the beauty of our lives streaming by in Morgana and elsewhere.' In an interview much closer to the time she actually wrote the stories, she spoke of her motivation: 'It has something to do with the fight against death, the feeling that we lose everything every day, and writing is a way of convincing yourself perhaps that you're doing something about this.'[31] And so, in writing these key stories, Munro was not simply returning to root her imagination in place, to invent an anchoring concreteness, as a way of having a uniform setting for a variety of stories, she was simultaneously finding a voice for her intimate sense of death, a sense of loss, and the fierce desire to make the passing moment significant in the larger shape of a lifetime.

This is even more evident in her remarks on James Agee's final novel, published posthumously in 1955. 'I read *A Death in the Family* and was enormously moved. That probably comes as close to what I mean by the art which doesn't feel artful, though it is not at *all* a naturalist book. The technique just seems to me transparent. It was one of the most powerful books in personal terms, in the way of thinking "I want to be able to write like that," that I ever read.'[32] She goes on to speak of specific moments that are treated in a low key, artless way, 'not fictionalizing'. The book appears to have made her conscious, perhaps for the first time, of how much plot and drama can be dispensed with, so that 'reality' dictates by itself what is going to happen in the writing. 'By reality I don't mean the reality I see. I mean the reality you feel.' She went on to read and admire *Let Us Now Praise Famous Men*, and found similarly affecting descriptions there; significantly, she remarked, 'The description of the interior of the sharecropper's house is to me one of the most important things I've ever read.' But apart from the intimacy with his characters' immediate experience that Agee made possible, *A Death in the Family* revealed to her a subject and a method that would become the foundation of her 'personal' writing.

~

This was made manifest for the first time in 'The Peace of Utrecht', which she wrote in 1959. Munro believes it marks her breakthrough as a writer of fiction, the 'most important story' in her debut collection. It was 'the first story I absolutely had to write and wasn't writing to see if I could write that kind of story'.[33] Then, she told J. R. (Tim) Struthers, her interviewer in 1982, 'I saw that writing was about something else altogether than I had expected it was, that it was going to be less in my control and more inescapable than I had thought.' The story 'came out of my mother's death', she continued. 'Until my mother dies, though the relationship with her was a very painful, deep one, I wasn't able to look at it or think about it.' The subject is approached indirectly, the search for a narrative voice a struggle to come to terms with the material of tragedy, and, indeed, it might be said, to simultaneously find a voice for the silenced and now deceased mother.

The story arose out of the circumstances of her mother's prolonged illness and death, and on one level it is an exploration of how much of the reality of pain, physical and emotional, can be captured in language. More specifically, when Helen—the Munro character—returns to the childhood home to share her grief with her sister, who has stayed to care for their mother, they discover that they do not really have a language in which to talk about her, or about their own lives. Munro invents a way to investigate layers of grief in the haunted house of her childhood. In the process of exploring indirectly the depths of the mother–daughter relationship, she also discovered a way to reveal patterns that keep in suspense the irresolution of major events in a lifetime. However powerful the desires that shape particular relationships and events, and shape the stories that bring them to life, the autobiographical undercurrent touches deeper realities of the intractability of circumstances. The limitations of language as a means of intimate communication between family members underline the tragic mode Munro is working in here, and so the searching personal voice in which the first-person narrator addresses the reader is what Munro can no longer avoid.

In 'The Peace of Utrecht', a tone of detachment, perhaps more appropriate to a memoir or essay, dramatizes the distance and silence between the two sisters, the 'determinedly undismayed' Maddy, and the narrator, who fears that when the visit ends, 'we will have to look straight into the desert that is between us'.[34] The opening pages sketch the new life of Maddy following her mother's death, her partying life with a group of women approaching middle-age, and her friendship with a married man; it emerges that the narrator has been absent for a considerable length of time, is married and has children. Regarding her friendship with the married man, whose wife is an invalid, Maddy remarks that 'he speaks the same language' and 'nobody else does'.[35] Helen has become estranged not only from her sister and her own past but from the provincial culture of her childhood; she learns how much of an outsider she has become in her bid to make a free life away from her first home. She learned in adolescence that the 'holiday world of school, of friends, and, later on, of love' can replace the 'dim world of continuing disaster, of home'. Now she wants to ask her sister 'is it possible that children growing up as we did lose the ability to believe in—to be at home in—any ordinary and peaceful reality'.[36] Such a conversation is impossible with Maddy, but there is a hint here that Munro has discovered why 'home', a 'peaceful reality', will have to be a state constructed in the language of art.

Helen is slowly overwhelmed by memories of her mother. 'I was allowing myself to hear—as if I had not dared before—the cry for help—undisguised, oh, shamefully undisguised and raw and supplicating that sounded in her voice.'[37] It is surely this cry that she cannot share with her sister, for both of them developed a way of protecting themselves from the bewilderment of grief. 'Never for a moment was there a recognition of the real state of affairs, never a glint of pity to open the way for one of her long debilitating sieges of tears.' Worse still, their 'parodies of love' led them to be 'unfailing in cold solicitude; we took away from her our anger and impatience and disgust, took all emotions away from our dealings with her, as you might take away meat from a prisoner to weaken him, till he died'. The narrator's unsparing examination of her adolescent self continues as she sifts through memories of her mother's ways of grappling with her decline, but it is now clear that her strategy of distancing herself from her mother and from the community left her numb to the tragic enormity of her mother's refusal to accept her fate and of her own limited ability to offer love.

When Helen tries to share with Maddy a memory of her mother before the illness struck, however, her sister dismisses this 'cowardly tender nostalgia, trying to get back to a gentler truth': 'I think you would have to have been away...to get those kind of memories.'[38] The years that Maddy spent caring for her mother have left her with no earlier memories, nor, it seems, any desire to retrieve them, whereas Helen, searching for the truth embedded in memories, as in this new, overwhelming revelation of her mother's and her sister's later lives, appears to have an epiphany that opens a way towards 'peace'. It may be that what she discovers is a self-as-writer that allows her to acknowledge the truth of what happened in her mother's life and the truth of her own estrangement, neither of them truths that can be articulated outside fiction.

In writing this story, it is as if Munro came to realize how she had wanted to evade the tragic material of her mother's life, to escape the 'cry' hidden inside the mother's inarticulate efforts to communicate. 'I didn't want to be tainted by tragedy', she remarked later of this period of her youth; 'I didn't want to live in a tragedy.'[39] Only when Helen discovers that her mother had briefly escaped from the home Maddy had put her in during her final period does her sympathy for her mother overwhelm her, for she, unlike her mother, had succeeded in running away. She suggests to Maddy that she too might consider leaving the home place to find another, new, life, but Maddy realizes she cannot leave.

Munro's story represents indirectly her effort to embrace the tragic material of her mother's life and of her own, to find a voice for her mother whose disease has reduced her to inarticulacy. In identifying to a degree with her mother's lack of a language in which to communicate, her imprisonment in silence, the burden the artist feels compelled to assume is to find a voice for herself that will acknowledge that reality of suffering and grief; in dramatizing the visit home, she discovers a new depth in her own writing voice and a new value in the material of her mother's life and of home. 'From then on', Munro remarked in 1972, 'this was the only kind of story I wrote',[40] meaning, I believe, that the 'real life', the only material for fiction she now valued, had to have a depth that she began to call 'personal'.

~

Many years after writing 'The Peace of Utrecht', Munro echoed Henry James and others[41] when she spoke of how she reads stories and also of how she writes her own: 'I don't take up a story and follow it as if it were a road, taking me somewhere.... It's more like a house. Everybody knows what a house does, how it encloses space and makes connections between one enclosed space and another and presents what is outside in a new way.'[42] It is as if the writing of 'The Peace of Utrecht', the return to her home and its many rooms and contrasting voices, provided her with a model from which she drew an aesthetic orientation and method. Regarding her own writing, she speaks of identifying a feeling, which she must then discover how to 'house' in a narrative structure: 'It's not a question of, "I'll make this kind of house because if I do it right it will have this effect." I've got to make, to build up, a house, a story, to fit around the indescribable "feeling" that is like the soul of the story.' Having moved from 'control' in her apprentice-ship phase to something approximating an 'inescapable' exploratory process, her house of fiction is grounded in memories and associations, often autobiographical images. This is a writing method moving deci-sively away from narrative oriented towards historical or biographical truth, and, indeed, from the larger, dramatic structures of a novel.

Somewhat surprisingly, it was not only the haunting presence of her mother in her childhood home that inspired Munro to think of her art as a method for connecting different kinds of feeling. Although it is unclear how conscious she was of this method while writing 'The Peace of Utrecht', it is evident that the various 'rooms' in that story are arranged in contrasting voices or ways of communicating; Helen's and Maddy's, to begin with, but then, very significantly, the mother's and others. The narrator contrasts in recollection her mother's rational mentality, reflected in conversation that is linear, direct, 'a cruel light', with the mentality of her paternal grandmother and grand-aunt, more subtle, more like 'weaving'; yet their disapproval could be 'like tiny razor cuts, bewilderingly, in the middle of kindness'. Munro introduces these figures again in various stories, long after 'The Peace of Utrecht', but in *Lives of Girls and Women* Aunt Elspeth and Aunt Grace are contrasted with Munro's mother in striking ways. 'My mother went along straight lines. Aunt Elspeth and Auntie Grace wove in and out around her....There was a whole new language to learn in their house. Conversations there had many levels, nothing could be stated directly, every joke might be a thrust turned inside out.'[43] This radical contrast between 'enclosed spaces' is reflected in the irreconcilable contrast between Helen and Maddy in 'The Peace of Utrecht', and indeed this distance between styles of expression, between mothers and daughters, men and women, and friends, occupied Munro repeatedly from this time on. The 'whole new language' she says she learns from these older women sounds very like the characteristic Munrovian combination of voices and perspectives, the gentle and the grotesque, the compassionate and the ironic.

After 'The Peace of Utrecht', Munro went on to complete fourteen volumes in more than half a century of writing, all of which she insists are stories, not memoirs, even when she admits that autobiographical feeling is the 'soul' of the story. Long after writing that story, Munro commented: 'The material about my mother is my central material in life, and it always comes the most readily to me.'[44] In context, that may be true, and there are many stories in which the mother image figures, notably in very well-known stories, in the decades after *Lives*, such as 'The Ottawa Valley', 'Chaddeley and Flemings: 1. Connection', 'The Progress of Love' and 'Friend of my Youth'. However, there are also many stories that focus on the father, and in retrospect, it is instructive to note how 'Utrecht' is imagined without the father: Robert Laidlaw was present throughout his wife's long illness and in 1959 was still living in Munro's childhood home, but she deliberately excluded a father's presence from the fiction so that its 'soul' could be preserved and those voices allowed to articulate a chorus of female selves.

～

Dance of the Happy Shades was dedicated to Robert Laidlaw, and the opening story is 'Walker Brothers Cowboy'; it appears that for a time Munro wished the collection to be given this title rather than naming it after a story written in 1961. 'Walker Brothers Cowboy' was written in late 1967 and it serves as a prologue to the collection; in turn, the

brief opening scene acts as a prologue to the story, a method of indirection Munro often used.

This rather formal scene focuses on an evening walk undertaken by
father and young daughter to Lake Huron.[45] 'Want to go down and see
if the Lake's still there?' the father invites her, his humour immediately
contrasting with the daughter's evident irritation with her mother,
who is 'making clothes for me' from discarded clothes of her own. Her
brother wishes he could accompany them out of the house, but it is
evident that this is a private moment for father and daughter, away
from the mother and the house. They walk through town streets, the
daughter noting everything as they go: 'Children, of their own will,
draw apart, separate into islands of two or one under the heavy trees,
occupying themselves in such solitary ways as I do all day, planting
pebbles in the dirt or writing in it with a stick.'[46] Told in the first person and present tense, the girl's childhood recollection has an understated autobiographical intensity, the memory becoming timeless and
dreamlike in creating a scene which is finally more about the experience of time than of place, and there may even be a distant Proustian
echo in its introductory role in relation to the collection.[47]

The father emerges as a calm and benign figure, in marked contrast
to the mother, and this contrast and the elaboration of the father's
character becomes the formal focus of the narrative later, but to begin
with the focus is on time. Continuing the slow walk down streets the
narrator partially recalls, the pair eventually reach the lakeshore already
known to the girl. But on this occasion, the father 'tells me how the
Great Lakes came to be'. Evoking a landscape in geological time, he
explains how the Ice Age created the landscape in the arrival of the ice
and then in its retreat created the lakes. 'They were *new*, as time went.
I try to see that plain before me, dinosaurs walking on it, but I am not
able even to imagine the shore of the Lake when the Indians were
there, before Tuppertown. The tiny share we have of time appals me,
though my father seems to regard it with tranquillity.'[48] She is puzzled
by the father's ability to grasp this expansive sense of time, a scientific
sense of human existence in an eternal perspective, although his experience of historical changes even in the twentieth century is limited. 'He
was not alive when this century started. I will be barely alive—old,
old—when it ends. I do not like to think of it.' She wishes to arrest
time, to evade the experience of ageing and mortality, and is intrigued
by her father's calm acceptance of the present without anguish. The

remainder of the story investigates that puzzle of the father's character, and, implicitly, she comes to know him by uncovering a part of his life before he married, and through observing him relate to a woman he had been attracted to, who contrasts sharply with the girl's mother.

Before the visit to Nora Cronin at her farm in the countryside some distance from their own home, the father, a salesman for Walker Brothers' drugstore, drives through the countryside, stopping at farms, soliciting business. The drive, echoing to a degree the walk to the Lake, begins with the girl's 'rising hope of adventure', and she is not disappointed as her father laughs much of the time and sings comic songs he has made up, many of them featuring himself as a 'Cowboy'. His lightheartedness is overshadowed in the girl's reflections by the opposing figure of her mother: 'That is not my mother's idea of a drive in the country',[49] and the walk with the father is also contrasted to a walk to town with her mother: 'We have not walked past two houses before I feel we have become objects of universal ridicule.' She does not want to be associated with her mother's 'bitterness, with no reconciliation', with her depressing sense of their personal 'calamity': 'I loathe even my name when she says it in public, in a voice so high, proud and ringing, deliberately different from the voice of any other mother on the street.' The girl has withdrawn her sympathy from her mother, and is now 'wary of being trapped into sympathy or any unwanted emotion'. She notes her father's buoyancy out on the road and, referring to the death of the salesman whose job her father has now, she comments: 'my father's voice is mournful-jolly, making his death some kind of nonsense, a comic calamity'.[50] In the voices of the mother and father, she detects the spirit of tragedy and the spirit of comedy.

The visit to Nora is a joyous occasion, marked by much laughter, joking, and dancing, and the girl notes that among the father's transgressions of the mother's rules is the drinking of a glass of whisky. This is a space beyond the mother's influence: 'Nora's dress...is flowered more lavishly than anything my mother owns.'[51] Mesmerized by her father's freedom to enjoy himself and Nora's equally spontaneous rapport with him, the girl observes everything in the present tense, and then she notes a picture of the Virgin Mary on the wall: 'I knew that such pictures are found only in the homes of Roman Catholics and so Nora must be one.'[52] This afternoon is also a cultural initiation for her because the families of her mother and father do not socialize with Catholics; she recalls the bigoted aura of an expression, '*She digs with the wrong foot'*, used by her paternal grandmother and aunt, and realizes this is how Nora would be categorized and, perhaps, that this is the reason her father's relationship with Nora had ended. The girl is surprised how comfortable she feels with this woman, so unlike her mother: 'Round and round the linoleum, me proud, intent, Nora laughing and moving with great buoyancy, wrapping me in her strange gaiety, her smell of whisky, cologne, and sweat.'[53] This earthy, vital force is given full expression, and there is only a hint of bitterness when Nora remarks, 'Time...will you come by ever again?' and as they leave, 'She touches the fender, making an unintelligible mark in the dust there.'[54] It is a clear echo of the opening scene in which the children in their 'solitary ways' write in the dust and of the girl's anxiety about time.

As they drive home towards the 'overcast' weather by the lake, she knows she will not disclose anything to her mother and enters into a kind of conspiracy with her father to protect his private pleasure on this afternoon. She has gained a new sense of how the present moment may offer such intense experiences of joy and pleasure, and of how reconnecting with such past moments, and their reliving, as it were, situates her in a creative and vital relationship with time and memory. There is a powerful imaginative awakening associated here with the figure of the father:

I feel my father's life flowing back from our car in the last of the afternoon, darkening and turning strange, like a landscape that has an enchantment on it, making it kindly, ordinary and familiar while you are looking at it, but changing it, once your back is turned, into something you will never know, with all kind of weathers, and distances you cannot imagine.[55]

Again, there is an echo in this last phrase of the girl's inability at the lake to imagine her father's expansive sense of time and eternity, but, in fact, the energy coming from deep, joyous feeling is the central aspect of 'real life' discovered here.

'Walker Brothers Cowboy' is a portrait of the artist as a young girl, and she awakens to an enchantment in her father's character, an imaginative power as singer and humorous talker. She feels something that cannot be rendered in expository prose, but she has absorbed all the atmospheres attached to images and to the voices of her mother, her father, and Nora. She intuits their contrasting essential selves and the limits to their communication of these selves. The intense form of communication she comes to know by being with her father and Nora on this day is set against the solitary state in which people try to write messages in the dust, to preserve and affirm their own selfhood in the brief time available.

∽

This sense of an embedded portrait of the artist and of a style moving towards even greater confidence and clarity is evident in 'Images', the story written more or less simultaneously with 'Walker Brothers Cowboy', and both stories are explicitly linked to *Lives of Girls and Women* by naming the father in both stories 'Ben Jordan' and using the first-person narrative voice of his young daughter. Munro has said that 'I like that short story the best', and at this same time, 1971/72, she wrote a spirited riposte to a crudely reductive reading of 'Images', and, in the process, provided some key insights into her method in this breakthrough phase. Rejecting the assumptions that she consciously intended an image taken from her experience to be read symbolically, and that her work is either a transcription of memories or a schematically planned construct, she wrote:

It has actually become difficult to sort out the real memories—like the house—used in this story from those that are not 'real' at all. I think the others are real because I did not consciously plan, make or arrange them; I found them. And it is all deeply, perfectly true to me, as a dream might be true, and all I can say, finally, about the making of a story like this is that it must be made in the same way our dreams are made.[56]

It is interesting, of course, that the 'symbol' that excited Munro's angry response was a house, because in 'Images' there is, indeed, a clear exemplification of her own sense of story as a house with its many rooms arranged around the 'soul' of the story.

The centre of consciousness is again the young girl, listening, observing, absorbing atmospheres and images in various contrasting spaces, and learning through an outing with her father how to accept her home situation and her ill mother with greater equanimity. The 'soul' of the story is the girl's fear because of her premonitions of impending death: 'I was not dreaming, I was trying to understand the danger, to read the signs of invasion.'[57] Clearly, while many of the fears might be considered to be those of a child, nourished by dreams and legends, the clarity of the girl's language has the discrimination of the artist-voice and her narrative is marked by images and observations that fall into complex implicit passages of repetition and contrast. In view of her commentary quoted earlier, the method of inventing a real truth relies on vivid memories that are not quite memories and a sense of how dreaming and understanding are closely allied. The voice of the child-narrator is, then, a complex invention, its naïvety a kind of wisdom, and again the father's world and his voice are significantly set against the room the mother occupies. The child's fears are moderated by his calm presence.

The mother's world of illness is introduced indirectly by the lingering death of the child's grandfather a year earlier, and now the mother seems to have taken his place. The two characters are linked by a nurse, a paternal cousin, who has cared for dying relatives, and she has now 'invaded' their house and the girl's fear is heightened by her presence. 'My mother's my grandmother's my aunts' voices wove their ordinary repetitions', but now the girl is conscious that 'all this real life going on' is different and the house seems permeated by 'the fact of death-contained, that little lump of magic ice'.[58] The nurse, she imagines, 'gloomy as an iceberg herself, implacable, waiting and breathing. I held her responsible.' She finds her voice 'loud and hoarse', her presence experienced as an oppression not only of her but of her mother also: 'If she had never come my mother would never have taken to her bed.' It is the logic of a child, but she is reading the 'signs of invasion' in her own way. She notices that her father too seems to have changed, but in his case, having a family cousin present appears to have released in him 'family ways', subdued in his marriage, such as teasing and laughter and practical joking.

When her father invites her to 'come with me and look at the traps'—traplines he has set by the river to catch muskrats—she feels released to go with him and welcomes the chance to enter his 'places where our judgment could not follow', referring to herself and her mother. In fact, her first significant initiation is to a dead muskrat: 'I only wanted, but did not dare, to touch the stiff, soaked body, a fact of death.'[59] The landscape now seems to reflect the girl's sense of governing forces, 'the wind... its own invading shape', the noise of the river coming from 'some hidden place where the water issued with a roar from underground'. Suddenly, she sees among the trees a mysterious man carrying an axe and heading towards her father, but she 'is not paralyzed by fear': 'This is the sight that does not surprise you, the thing you have always known was there that comes so naturally, moving delicately and contentedly and in no hurry, as if it was made, in the first place, from a wish of yours, a hope of something final, terrifying.' This image of a marauding agent of death is, surprisingly, greeted by her father: 'I heard my father's voice come out, after a moment's delay, quiet and neighbourly.' Joe, who lives in the woods, invites them to his house, a half-burned-down structure that he has roofed over, and it is this 'house' that a critic had interpreted as a symbol of burial. More significant is the fear that grips Joe, for he believes that his enemies burned down his house; he is both an image out of a fairy tale, in the girl's imagination, and also a victim of his own imagined fears, and so somewhat like the girl herself.

The father comforts him, and reassures him that enemies are not about to attack him, and in reassuring him he also reassures his daughter. On the way back from this initiation in the woods, he points out to her in the distance another house that she recognizes as their own. He cautions her not to mention her terror of the man with the axe to her mother and the nurse. 'They might be scared about it', he cautions her; 'you and me aren't, but they might be'.[60] At home, the girl realizes that she is 'no longer afraid' of the nurse or indeed of what she had become the sign of. Her father jokes that Joe might be a possible partner for the nurse, and the girl remains quiet, as he had requested, while he tells his story of their adventure. The narrative voice, absorbing the father's playful and flexible imagination, concludes: 'Like the children in fairy stories who have seen their parents make pacts with terrifying strangers, who have discovered that our fears are based on nothing but the truth . . . like them, dazed and powerful with secrets, I never said a word.' The dreams and the truth of the girl's experience—a secret from her mother—surely exemplify the 'real' that Munro insisted was the story's style, and the manner in which the girl's consciousness is embedded in the adult narrative voice exemplifies Munro's mature method.

In *Lives of Girls and Women*, Munro moves from the farm and bush and, as Del enters the adult world alone, seems to embrace this parallel world that is deeply rooted in daily life in Jubilee. No longer an observing child, she is drawn into the drama and the responsibility of intimate action, and so the intensity of the domestic relationships and voices of 'The Peace of Utrecht' becomes rooted in this wider world. Each of the succeeding volumes will experiment with time and remembering, the recapturing of specific places and specific historical periods,[61] and there are stories that go back over the material of childhood. Most strikingly, perhaps, in the concluding story of *Something I've Been Meaning to Tell You*, Munro writes once more of her mother and concludes in the voice of a writer, commenting on the story she has created: 'I wanted to find out more, remember more, I wanted to bring back all I could. . . . it is to reach her that this whole journey has been undertaken. With what purpose? To mark her off, to describe, to illumine, to celebrate, to *get rid* of, her; and it did not work, for she looms too close, just as she always did.'[62] This is Munro's most overtly introverted statement, speaking of a deeply personal matter, and from this point on, the writer-voice is often included, taking the reader beyond the illusion of consistent narrative voice, or the voices of mother or father which so often were the most intensely remembered presences in that voice.

In 1973, Munro left the Canadian Pacific coast and returned to settle in that part of Ontario she had fled more than twenty years earlier. Soon after her return, she wrote a memoir/story called 'Home', about a visit to her father on the farm of her childhood. Inevitably, it recalls the earlier, created account of a visit to the house in 'The Peace of Utrecht', a story from which images of husband and father were entirely absent. Her father has remarried, and Munro herself has separated from her husband, has uprooted herself once more, and is beginning a new life. She is also beginning a new life as a writer, no longer focused so much on the material of Jubilee but on patterns of change and transformation, on the remaking of the self and fluid points of view, on what is hinted at in the title of her next collection, *Who Do You Think You Are?*

Apart from crude awakenings to material and visceral realities in the new life her father has made in the house, Munro's main discovery about her childhood home is that, while she was away, she 'was greatly moved by the memory of it', but now the transformed house has destroyed those memories. Her father assumes that it will still mean a lot to her: 'I don't tell him that I am not sure now whether I love any place, and that it seems to me it was myself I loved here—some self that I have finished with and none too soon.'[63] Munro seems to acknowledge that the personal self she had painfully dramatized in 'The Peace of Utrecht' is no longer true enough. It is a different relationship to the house and its memories that she seeks to imagine now. The voice she had found for looking back and creating an image of Jubilee and its environs a generation earlier now begins to assume not only an autobiographical dimension but a historical one, the history of a changing self and point of view. That sense of the dimensions of time entered 'Walker Brothers Cowboy', and later stories had made mutability a condition of the intensity of observation.

Published in Canada in 1974, 'Home' was the first of a series, which Munro did not collect until *The View from Castle Rock* in 2006. This is a collection of family history stories, which, she says, 'pay more attention to the truth of a life than fiction usually does',[64] and in her final collection, *Dear Life*, she also includes a set of autobiographical pieces. 'I was doing something closer to what memoir does—exploring a life, my own life, but not in an austere or rigorously factual way. I put myself in the centre and wrote about that self, as searchingly as I could.'[65] Not surprisingly, these final stories bring her back once more to memories of being in that first home.

In *Dear Life* she comes full circle, and this in the final paragraphs of the last story, 'Dear Life', the last words of her writing career. The four 'works' grouped in a section called 'Finale' are narratives of childhood, focused on the child's discovery of death, of irrational motivation, of love and sexuality, of the erosion of belief, but they also include portraits of her mother and father and reflect on roles they played in her life at this early stage. In the final paragraph, she confesses: 'I did not go home for my mother's last illness or for her funeral.'[66] It is evident that the painful 'soul' of 'The Peace of Utrecht' has stayed with her right to the end. 'We say of some things that they can't be forgiven, or that we will never forgive ourselves. But we do, we do it all the time.'

These last compassionate and ironic words of Munro's final volume are characteristic of the tone that always envelops self-awareness and the inner voice. The vision she discovered in writing the first story she 'had to write' was that dismay in the face of the irrational forces in life can be managed only by such compassionate stoicism. 'People have thoughts they'd sooner not have', her father had told her in 'Night', another of these last memoir-stories. 'It happens in life'; and she then comments on her father's comforting remark: 'It set me down, but without either mockery or alarm, in the world we were living in.'[67] That is the world Munro circles in all the stories following 'The Peace of Utrecht', and, as another of this final set of stories, 'Voices', reaffirms, the real life of her world is recalled and created through voices.

3

William Trevor's *Mrs Eckdorf in O'Neill's Hotel*

The lonely voice

William Trevor came to writing late and somewhat accidentally. In the mid-1950s, after leaving Ireland to work as a teacher and sculptor in various places in England, he wrote a novel 'for profit when I was very poor'.[1] *A Standard of Behaviour* was well received in London reviewing circles, but six years went by until he wrote what he considers his 'first serious novel', *The Old Boys*. At this stage, he was thirty-five, living in London and working in an advertising agency. The great success of this novel in 1964 launched him into a career as a writer of stories, plays, television dramas, and novels, three other novels being published in the 1960s.[2] His first volume of stories, *The Day We Got Drunk on Cake*, appeared in 1968. Thus began a career during which, in the next two decades alone, he wrote seven novels and six volumes of stories. Such extraordinary productivity and professional success reflect a distinctive and sure style, a vision and a sense of voice which are confidently grounded in a personal and independent view of the cultural significance of storytelling. John Banville has remarked that Trevor 'is almost unique among modern novelists in that his own voice is never allowed to intrude into his fictions', yet Banville continues to characterize 'his inimitable, calmly ambiguous voice' that 'can mingle in a single sentence pathos and humour, outrage and irony, mockery and love'.[3] In short, the complex vision and conflicting perceptions of life of the self-effacing artist permeate the persona of the storyteller who must present his readers 'with some kind of coherent story that works. It is a business of communication. ... That is a personal statement because I don't like abstract novels any more than I like abstract art.'[4] Although Trevor is to some degree, then, an old-fashioned storyteller, he eschews omniscience and guards against an intrusive authorial voice.

Trevor rarely speaks of his own work, and steadfastly refuses to analyse novels or stories, or to plot a narrative of his own development as an artist. In rare interviews, he insists that his writing is an intuitive activity and that he prefers to guard the mystery of how fictions take shape or how style is refined: 'I'm an instinctive writer...I have no messages or anything like that; I have no philosophy and I don't impose on my characters anything more than the predicament they find themselves in....I don't know how I do it. And I believe that mystery is essential.'[5] The mystery and the freedom that he says underlie his work method—appearing here to generalize from his experience as a writer of stories rather than novels—are also qualities Trevor grants to his characters and his readers. The narrator appears to have a light hand in the telling of the story, yet the 'predicament [the characters] find themselves in' sets the limits to the drama and indeed is often the same limitation that different characters in different circumstances must face. One critic commented on the shift from the Dickensian aspect of the early work 'in the direction of the pessimistic, if not exactly the Hardyesque', towards a 'vision, as dark in its way as the fatalism that informs *Tess of the d'Urbervilles* or *Jude the Obscure*', and Trevor himself spoke of the difficulty he would have choosing between Dickens and Hardy if he had to select one.[6] Speaking of craft, he remarks, 'You write. The reader imagines: your task is to control the relationship.'[7] And elsewhere: 'You must have confidence in your skill as a craftsman, I think. Not confidence that you're going to be right every time; but you have to be confident in saying to yourself, "Only I really know how this works, because I made it."'[8] There is, then, less freedom inherent in the human material and in how the imagination elaborates the material than Trevor suggests. All his characters share a common set of predicaments, and the vision of life which is revealed in his approach to them underlies the unmistakable voice of Trevor, the storyteller.[9]

The early work won much praise for the precision of its style and accuracy of its observation, its comic and satirical portrayal of marginal individuals, and its dark sense of lurking malevolence and concealed suffering which often led to grotesque and even violent behaviour. *The Boarding House* is perhaps most eloquent in articulating this grotesque sense of a dysfunctional urban community. These qualities, somewhat gothic and melodramatic, remain in some of the later fiction, but the maturity of voice and vision which led to his international recognition as one of the great writers of the age, are grounded on a major shift in emphasis on storytelling, and on a set of convictions about his artistic identity which emerged at the end of the apprentice-ship phase of the 1960s. From this point on, his career developed along a number of separate paths, notably as a novelist and as a writer of short stories, and his sense of the scope of the two genres as distinct modes of storytelling certainly shaped that development.

Mrs Eckdorf in O'Neill's Hotel, published in 1969, and a number of short stories written just before and after mark this change. All Trevor's fiction up to this point had been set in England. He has explained that the need to understand the society he had settled in was a major moti-vating force for his acute observation and listening, although, more generally, he says he writes to understand people who are different from him, such as old people, women, and children. He insists he has no interest in introspection and always looks out to understand the world's strangeness. In the late 1960s, he turned to find material in another society that was also strange to him, or at least, it was now strange because in writing about England, he had learned how to observe from an outsider's perspective. The other society was Ireland, the place of his birth and education, which he had left in his early twenties. 'I have no roots', he said, appearing to embrace exile and the ambiguous outsider role in both England and Ireland, which he said facilitates the 'distance' necessary for art.[10] After fifteen years away, however, and after he had left London to become a full-time writer and settled in the Devon countryside, he 'found that Ireland was falling into perspective'.[11]

Excursions in the Real World provides a sketch of his familial and social contexts as a child.[12] His parents were not Catholic, but neither did they belong to the traditional category of the Protestant Ascendancy or landed gentry, nor did they believe that Ireland was not their home country. His father worked as a bank official, and so the family moved frequently to different towns in Ireland as his father was promoted, but Trevor, inclined towards a benign view, notes that his father was a gre-garious man who related easily to his largely Catholic clients. Hence, as a child, Trevor changed homes and schools many times, eventually, in adolescence, becoming a boarder at two Protestant schools in Dublin. These geographical displacements and the lack of a stable set of friends and neighbours, or extended family, made Trevor an avid reader and cinema-goer, but neither reading nor the cinema reflected the society in which he was living; they provided welcome means of escape for his mother and, then, for him. While the essays register a real attachment to Irish places, landscapes, and townscapes, and a sympathetic awareness of the cultural inheritance of sectarian and imperial histories, they focus on individuals most of all and on ways in which beliefs, fantasies, and religious visions can permeate an individual consciousness for good or ill.

In a way, it was the other Ireland, the strange Ireland, he wanted to understand in this new fiction, the Ireland of his own past, and, more generally, to understand how the past determines the present. More than this, it was indirectly an effort to understand how he himself belonged there or at least in what sense he felt 'Irish', as he insists he does in spite of decades living in England. The effort to understand how his imagination may have been shaped there led to a consideration of Irish writing and how the culture had distinctive literary traditions. In later years, Trevor described himself as a 'religious novelist' and remarked that, while he does not practise any religion, 'God-bothering' is a preoccupation; this first 'purely Irish novel' is centrally preoccupied with varieties of Catholic belief and practice.[13] But it also situates religious forms of hope and conviction in a wider consideration of narrative transformations of the ordinary, such as in art. This complex novel was certainly not written in his usual intuitive way, for, over the years, he became increasingly self-conscious about how he belonged to an Irish literary tradition and articulated ideas that map an imaginative relocation and a maturity of style dating from *Mrs Eckdorf in O'Neill's Hotel*. It is not accidental that the stories written at this time and collected in 1972 as *The Ballroom of Romance* include his first stories set in Ireland or that the title story is considered one of a handful of his greatest stories. Trevor's imaginative engagement with Irish material in the late 1960s deeply affected the practice of his art of fiction for the remainder of his career.

Although William Trevor has described in an offhand manner the writing of his first novel and then the first stories which were published in 1962 and 1963, the making of art had been at the centre of his life since late adolescence. He has suggested that an interest in serious literature, in work by Joyce, George Eliot, Maugham, and Dickens, began around the age of sixteen, following many years of reading the popular novels his mother read, and that he remained a reader of literature from that time. He studied History, desultorily, at Trinity College, Dublin, and in the years after graduation, he taught at a secondary school, English being one of his subjects, but in fact, beginning in his adolescence and up to the age of thirty, sculpture was the art that interested him, in many different materials, wood, metal, clay, and sometimes stone. It is surely important to consider how this first artistic apprenticeship may have prepared the way for the work he would do, and how he would do it, when he turned to literature as his medium.

Oisín Kelly, a teacher in St Columba's boarding school, was his mentor and model, an individualistic artist and indifferent teacher who went on to become a celebrated sculptor. An essay in *Excursions* tells of Trevor's first assignment, to carve an eagle in wood, and the first challenge was to learn how to use the tools and gain control over the material: 'The grain was a pattern to make use of, a means of suggesting concavity or depth, an emphasis when you wanted it to be.'[14] Kelly did not believe the making of art could be taught, but in welcoming the schoolboy to his studio and allowing the young Trevor to observe him at work, he offered encouragement that inspired many years of dedication to the visual arts. During his time at Trinity, Trevor associated mostly with former school-friends outside the university, some of them painters or designers, but one detail from his time there is surely significant for the kind of novels he would later design. In the Long Room of the Library, the Book of Kells is displayed, one page turned each day so that the intricate Celtic artwork in the illuminated gospels may be seen in its full extent. He went there regularly to study this early form of visual art, to make sketches of its details, and it is notable that, years later, he carved 'its three evangelists as panels for a lectern in a village church in England'.[15] The Book of Kells was not the only work of religious art that interested Trevor, and much of his later employment in England was in making art for churches. For a time, however, in Dublin, he created work that was exhibited in galleries and exhibitions, such as the annual Irish Exhibition of Living Art. One of his pieces was exhibited at the Tate Gallery in London. In 1956, he returned from England for a solo exhibition in a Dublin gallery. The newspaper report on the opening and a subsequent review note that many of the pieces in a variety of materials and styles are religious in theme—'The Risen Christ', 'The Devil Appearing to Christ in the Wilderness', and 'Death of Saint Andrew' among them.

He left the West country, however, and moved to London to find work in an advertising agency. By the end of the decade 'the work had become abstract', Dolores MacKenna reports, 'and he was no longer happy with the effect'.[16] Although he wishes to leave abstraction in sculpture behind him, just as he says he became a storyteller so that a narrative reference could be preserved for readers, nevertheless his fiction maintains qualities not primarily realistic:

Being a sculptor does help you to form things. There's a way in which you think as a sculptor. You see things in the round very much.... And I've found that I still think like that when I'm writing. I'm still obsessed by form and pattern—the actual shape of things, the shape of a novel or the shape of a short story.[17]

Trevor's critical terminology is somewhat opaque, but his attempt here to articulate the feeling of composition suggests that while the observation of surfaces with an intensely curious eye is essential, equally vital is a sense of how realism is given other dimensions in the reader's imagination, such as moral fable, the supernatural, and story itself.

His many years of experimental work in the fine arts were, naturally, accompanied by an immersion in art history and in contemporary practice. While the intricacy of his interweaving of many lives in a kind of spacial art—in the novels of the 1960s, and in the 1970s, in *Elizabeth Alone* and *The Children of Dynmouth*, for instance—may owe something to his interest in the Book of Kells, in three-dimensional designs, and in depth in painting, what remained especially were work habits. He refers to Henry Moore as an ideal artist in his self-effacement and his dedication to his work as a sculptor. Even when literary language became Trevor's medium, he speaks of writing in terms that suggest carving and building, representation and abstraction, allowing the work to find a shape by a process of leaving in and taking out material. 'I experiment all the time but the experiments are hidden. Rather like abstract art: you look at an abstract picture, and then you look at a close-up of a Renaissance painting and find the same abstraction.'[18] He speaks of 'the perspective that art demands',[19] the 'distance', and when he wrote about revisiting places in Ireland he had known, what he values is not nostalgia or recollection but 'a lesson in proportion, an exercise in give and take'.[20] In interviews Trevor often uses analogies from the fine arts to suggest something about the nature of fiction: 'A novel is like a cathedral and you can't really carry in your imagination the form a cathedral is to take';[21] 'I think of a short story very much as a portrait';[22] 'If the novel is like an intricate Renaissance painting, the short story is an Impressionist painting.'[23] In the fiction, there are many references to specific paintings and visual images, including films, and this reinforces the sense of art as something made, neither self-expressive nor autobiographical.

If Trevor left sculpture behind as an avocation and turned to writing stories and novels in the 1960s, he was experienced in making art through an 'intuitive' process that excluded all introspection or theoretical ideas. He had a very practical sense of how to work, and his material lay all around him, for he was motivated, he insists, by curiosity. He went from being a reader of Waugh, Greene, and other established novelists of the 1950s in England to being a writer of fiction that resembled theirs in certain respects, but if he was an outsider collecting details as a journalist or a detective does to make a story, to get at a truth or unravel an enigma, this is only part of the method. He is drawn to observing individuals unlike himself, he has said, and in the 1960s he was also drawn to popular culture, to the songs, the fashions, the advertising that permeate the spiritual and emotional environment in which his individuals are imprisoned, even as they crave release and some kind of empowerment. His years in London, before settling in the countryside, appear to have given him not only material for fiction but also a vision of a wasteland, and gaining the necessary distance of art required more than a satirical detachment.[24]

An essay on Assia Weevil, included in *Excursions in the Real World*,[25] offers a deeper insight into how Trevor's characteristic style was being formed. In the essay, he recalls a figure for whom he had been a confidant in London in the early 1960s. So many aspects of Weevil's character as he describes her suggest that she and her milieu, and more generally, the 'swinging sixties' of London at that time contributed greatly to the vision of urban culture the early novels depict. Weevil had become the lover of Ted Hughes in the year before Sylvia Plath killed herself, but Trevor avoids discussing this biographical matter; instead, he focuses on a deft evocation of the personality Weevil had invented for herself, the instability and homelessness that underlay it, and the desperation that would eventually lead her to kill her child and herself. Trevor's brief portrait is an understated and restrained evocation of something grotesque and tragic in Weevil's life and in the culture of the time; the older Trevor, author of the essay, is compassionate and horrified. It is clear that in those years working in the advertising agency, he listened well and observed; the humour and the fantastical elements of the novels have a satirical edge, but it appears that growing below the distracting surfaces was a darker and troubled vision. If Trevor outgrew his work as a sculptor, in part because it had become too abstract, it might be suggested that he also outgrew his early writing because it had become too easy to simply repeat the satirical depiction of a dark and disillusioned urban world.

In a sense, then, early novels such as *The Old Boys* and *The Boarding House* are constructed as an eccentric group portrait, each character's life almost like a short story embedded for a time in the random grouping that assembled in a particular location, such as a boarding house or a school. William Trevor is interested most of all in how they make sense of their own lives, how they remember and desire and hope, how their past has shaped their present unawares. These fictions are not historical in any sense, nor will he become preoccupied with communal historical inheritances, in addition to personal inheritance, until he writes *Fools of Fortune* a decade later. But he has begun to work in ways that will situate a particular era such as the 1960s, and, later, certain periods in Irish history, in the wider concerns that his fiction-making will address. Although the conception of Ivy Eckdorf may owe something to Assia Weevil and her milieu in London, the technique and the vision have to be renewed. Trevor arrived at a point at which his thinking about the genres of fiction and his own past had to be reassessed.

In his earliest fictions, Trevor worked in a fluid medium in which he felt free to invent and experiment with narrative, so that the distinction of novel and short story was not simply generic, and, indeed, some of his fictions, such as *Reading Turgenev* and *Nights at the Alexandra*, are novellas. Later, he said that he is a writer of short stories who happens to write novels, and this distinction is important to him for the artistic priorities it appears to establish. He associates the novel, for the most part, with English social life, the short story with Ireland, and he will situate this distinction in a historical perspective. In the introduction to the *Oxford Book of Irish Short Stories* he refers to 'the civilized bookishness of writing novels and reading them' which he associates with middle-class English life, while Ireland remains 'an uneasy, and still largely peasant society' much given to oral storytelling.[26] Apart from his declared appreciation of Dickens, he views nineteenth-century English fiction as an art of a privileged and imperial mentality, and so his imagination was not drawn to the solid forms of realistic fiction descended from that tradition. Rather, his vision of a shifting and unstable world, shaped less by secure social structures than by isolated and marginal individuals, drew him to favour the short story, the genre of the 'glimpse', and to a kind of novel woven out of many glimpses. It is in this context that he would naturally turn to Joyce's method for the new novel of Dublin, and that the multiple stories and shifting points of view would be more than ever appropriate to his dark vision of life in the modern city. 'I'm very fond of Joyce', he remarked among numerous references to him, 'especially *Dubliners*',[27] and the many critics who have traced echoes and resemblances agree that it is the exiled Joyce's recreation of Dublin that interests Trevor, rather than Stephen Dedalus, *A Portrait of the Artist as a Young Man*, or Joyce's experiments in autobiographical fiction.

When Trevor turned to write his first novel set in Ireland, then, his craft was known and well-practised, his vision of life emerging. What was different was that *Mrs Eckdorf* was thematically and formally much more ambitious than the earlier books. He needed to enlarge and clarify a vision that would incorporate both the 'England' he had uncovered and the 'Ireland' he had known in a more intuitive way. There was a great deal he wanted to discover to satisfy his curiosity, for understanding Ireland was a more intimate need than what had driven him in his English fictions. In returning to Dublin, he was undoubtedly returning too to his own past when he lived in the city, and his main challenge was no longer observation for he could rely on memory and augment it. 'Born Irish I observe the world through Irish sensibilities',[28] he remarked some time after he wrote the novel, but it was the writing of the novel that clarified these 'sensibilities' for him. His main challenge was to find an appropriate voice or style to disclose the culture he had known through experience and yet was no longer living within. That voice would now embody those 'Irish sensibilities' and how the larger world might be observed through them.

~

The name of the hotel that is the location of the novel's realistic and symbolic actions is so unmistakably Irish that it alerts the reader to other implications of naming. The protagonist, Mrs Eckdorf, it is revealed in the opening pages, is not German, as one might expect, but a Londoner, from Maida Vale.[29] The run-down hotel in an old part of Dublin is situated on Thaddeus Street, Thaddeus being the apostle also known by the name Jude, patron of desperate cases, and hopelessness; while the hotel is no longer a commercial establishment, it does provide various kinds of shelter to many. The most significantly named character, however, is Mrs Sinnott, the owner of the hotel, a deaf and dumb woman in her nineties, who presides over the street from her upstairs window. Her daughter, her son and his estranged wife and son and many of the orphans she has fostered all visit her and write messages to her in the notebooks she has kept for years. An important figure in her immediate circumstances is O'Shea, one of her orphans and her long-time porter, who has become her primary care-giver, and through his eyes we are given the idea that Mrs Sinnott is a beatific presence, her hotel being to some degree a place of pilgrimage and a shrine to a secular saint. At the other end of the street lives Father Hennessey who spends his time writing a book on saints, although he wishes to demythologize the traditions of sainthood and the miraculous powers associated with them.

In fact, it is not only the hotel that has declined into poverty and squalor, for the surrounding neighbourhood and the city itself are impoverished, economically and in spirit. This motley population on Thaddeus Street is joined by casually encountered characters in the parks, streets, and quays of the city to convey an image that is surely an echo of an earlier literary treatment of the city. Trevor borrows many elements of *Dubliners* and *Ulysses* to remind the reader of the Joycean prototype of paralysis and dreams of alternative lives. In earlier novels, such as *The Boarding House*, he appeared to echo Dickens in his depiction of a cast of Londoners, for whom the stability of the house provides a haven for the homeless, or, at least, for individuals whose contingent lives compose a kind of urban kaleidoscope but not a community in any anchored sense. In that novel, he conveys an image of disconnected individuals mirroring one another in their deepest needs, isolated from each other and defensively protecting their privacy, their days passing simultaneously, their travelling around the city a metaphor for this contingency; and yet unexpected combinations of will and accident create connections between the characters. London and Dublin are similar in this sense of a grubby urban environment occupied by frustrated, lower middle-class characters, trapped in homes and offices, and a floating population of lonely individuals, imprisoned in a determined condition that is only alleviated by brief snatches of pleasure or fantasy. *Mrs Eckdorf in O'Neill's Hotel* is not merely a repetition of the method of *The Boarding House*; rather, it is a significant variation on it, and a radical movement away from its vision of life.

Trevor may have borrowed Joyce's technique from the 'Wandering Rocks' episode in *Ulysses* in the earlier novels, but in *Mrs Eckdorf* his similarity is singularly appropriate for this city that appears not to have changed since Joyce identified its condition as the state of paralysis. Hour by hour, characters make their way about the city, meeting and parting, preoccupied with their tasks, sometimes only with their fantasies and dreams, often simply passing the time in drinking, betting on horses, going to the dentist, or enjoying the perusal of recipes for cooking something new and interesting. The pimp, Morrissey, and his women wait for business, and, remarkably, it arrives eventually in the form of a visiting English businessman who has spent much of his day requesting the help of various barmen; clerks in an insurance office put in the hours at their desks; the ageing Father Hennessey continues to write his book on saints' lives; all of them are loosely connected by the chore of buying a birthday gift for Mrs Sinnott, and then by the birthday party which takes place in the hotel kitchen. They are also connected briefly by the arrival of Mrs Ivy Eckdorf.

Mrs Eckdorf is recognizably a desperate case from her opening words on the first page when she begins to tell her fellow passenger on a flight from London many details of her life-story and her reason for visiting Dublin. This grotesquely comic encounter occupies the first chapter and introduces the protagonist, although she is not encountered again until three chapters later, when the ordinary reality of the Dubliners, their place, their routines and rituals have been established. Ivy Eckdorf is a professional photographer who has had international success with a series of expensive coffee-table books, each one a study of people of 'local interest' in an exotic part of the world. Her suffering subjects have been of 'local interest' for tragic or disturbing reasons, but their story is documented in pictures that are valued and appreciated for their beauty by middle-class consumers of such photographic art. She has aggressively appropriated the situations of these lives and imposed on them a narrative that she insists is the truth. Her reason for visiting Dublin is to investigate the tragedy she believes happened at the hotel a generation earlier. Unknown to herself, she is in search of a belief or vision that will provide some transcending meaning; the devotion to 'art' and its implicit message of 'understanding' has provided this until now, but the hysteria that is evident from the first chapter indicates that she is heading towards a crisis.

The novel follows her progress until she realizes that what happened at the hotel was not the 'tragedy' she had anticipated; rather, her brief experience at the hotel leads her to a realization that she had been a false artist. 'She stood alone, then, in the centre of her bedroom, thinking that she had come in arrogance and treachery, the woman her life had made her.' Her documentary art was a projection of her own suffering on the lives of others, she realizes, and she discovers a new goal as artist; 'without knowing a thing about it, she had come so that she too might learn forgiveness. She would display now for all the hard world to see a human story that was her own story also. . . . On azure-tinted photogravure paper she would show the working of a forgotten God.'[30] She abandons her plans for this new book project, however, and indeed abandons any wish to continue her previous life as she throws all her personal belongings into the Liffey, including the clothes she has been wearing. She is taken to an asylum, where she claims to have died and to be happy in 'heaven'. She comes to believe that the beatific aura of Mrs Sinnott has created a place from which goodness emanates and is overcome by a kind of fundamental Christian faith.

In her new state of religious ecstasy, she attempted to confess her life-story to Father Hennessey, who was at first dismayed by her egocentric assertiveness.[31] He, like others on the street, viewed her as mentally deranged. In the final chapter, however, he visits her, as he now does every Tuesday, for she has become an enigma in his landscape of beliefs and personal salvation. He comes to feel that her life has something to offer him, some understanding of the state between sainthood and madness. Humbled by the spectacle of her withdrawal from the wealth and success she once possessed, and from the self-centred power she once wielded, he is alone in the attention he gives to Ivy Eckdorf. The false artist he had once accused of voyeurism and exploitation has chosen simplicity and a kind of monastic contemplation that restores the old priest's faith.

~

Mrs Eckdorf in O'Neill's Hotel appears to have an aspect of autobiography embedded in the allegory of the artist figure. Ivy Eckdorf is exposed as a detached and arrogant interpreter of humble lives which may not indeed conform to her representation of them, but she is then transformed from a person evading the meaninglessness of her own daily life into a person who discovers an absolute and literal form of Christian belief. Like an early Christian contemplative, she removes herself from the world. In a review of Brian Moore's novel *No Other Life* in 1993, Trevor began by admitting that 'the lives of the saints make fascinating reading'. He is neither a credulous believer in the powers ascribed to the saints, nor is he entirely sceptical in allowing rational explanations to deconstruct the legendary images of these saints; instead, he concludes that 'they are real because people have made them so, their long vanished feature (sic) alive in the imaginations they nourish, their strength the faith of the faithful, the marvels of their lives an inspiration.' He is sympathetic to the impulse that venerates these saints and to the nourishment offered to the imagination by religious beliefs, even if saints may be powerless to prevent evil from happening. 'Somewhere in the entanglements of exaggeration and myth there is a whispering insistence that human goodness is what matters most of all: however faint, it's a sound to honour with the benefit of the doubt.'[32] This Christian paradigm of beatitude, goodness and charity in action becomes, from *Mrs Eckdorf* on, the miraculous foundation of the novels that Trevor refers to as 'cathedrals'.

When Mrs Sinnott is introduced to the reader in *Mrs Eckdorf in O'Neill's Hotel*, she awakes and 'her mind immediately filled: she saw scenes in Venice and the faces of her two children at different times in their lives, and the face of her husband who had been shot in 1911.'[33] In her room she has many religious emblems; 'among them, and dominant, a painted copy of the Virgin in Baldovinetti's Annunciation, had seventy years ago come . . . from her mother'.[34] It is then revealed that her mother is Venetian and that she herself was brought to Venice by her young husband; it is also revealed that he had been 'killed in revolutionary action'. She has vivid recollections of religious art from her visit to Venice, and then an explanation is offered for the fact that she gave up using sign language, although her husband and children had learned it. 'She preferred the written messages because as the pencil moved slowly over the paper she imagined that for her visitors the room was as silent almost as it was for her: she drew her visitors into her tranquillity.'[35] Mrs Sinnott's 'tranquillity' is associated with the Italian images of her religious conviction, her choice of silence and the written word, it would seem, a kind of communication akin to art and a response to the killing of her husband in political engagement.

One of those who enters her tranquillity by writing in her notebook is Father Hennessey, whose book includes the life of St Attracta: '*We*

must skim the truth from pretty myth, Father Hennessey had written for
[Mrs Sinnott's] benefit alone. *There is plenty of truth in St Attracta.*[36]
If Father Hennessey represents one kind of writer in the novel, his
work—a piece of art criticism, it seems—is devoted to clarifying the
simple truth of saints' lives, freed from the accretions of myths that
enveloped them as miracle workers. This old priest's approach to truth
is obviously the opposite of Mrs Eckdorf's photography in her books.
Yet a later account of Father Hennessey's work introduces doubt about
his ability to seize this truth, or indeed about the usefulness of this
clearing away of 'myth' from the biographical facts. 'The truth about
any saint, he reflected, was particularly difficult to establish: saints went
to people's hearts, they became decorated with legend, as statues of
Our Lady were decorated with glass jewellery in Italian churches.'[37]
He remembers that Mrs Sinnott had written to him '*Venice is heaven*'.
The priest's doubts about his ability to separate this Italian-style ven-
eration from the biographical approach leads to an even greater doubt
about his ministry, that 'he was more at ease with dead saints than with
the ordinary living'.[38] Lost in the stories of the saints, he is troubled: 'if
the mysteries of the saints didn't matter, there was the implication in
his mind that the mysteries of the ordinary living did, and should be
solved.'[39] By the end of the novel, when he pays his weekly visit to
Mrs Eckdorf in the asylum, his devotion to her echoes her own devotion to Mrs Sinnott: 'he sometimes felt that he could listen to her
forever.... Such happiness he had never seen before.'[40] She tells him
that Mrs Sinnott 'is a legend now in the hotel, among the new people
who have come there, and among guests who happen to be staying.... In all the bustle of the hotel, she is not forgotten, just as she in
her time ordained that her husband who was shot and her own parents
were not forgotten either.'[41] These two women are joined in their
attainment of a vision of 'heaven' to set against the violence and aggression they have experienced: in their happiness and tranquillity, their
eccentric distancing from ordinary life marks them as akin to religious
figures in art or mythic figures in supernatural narratives. They are the
first such figures in Trevor's fiction, but there will be many others, notably in novels such as *Fools of Fortune*, *Reading Turgenev*, *Felicia's Journey*,
and *The Story of Lucy Gault*.

    Fools of Fortune has been admired as a novel which investigates
the impact on individual lives of recurring incidents of politically
motivated violence in Irish history. It is one in a series of fictions,

novels and short stories, written mostly in the 1980s, which reflect on passages in Anglo-Irish relations, from the Great Famine in 'The News from Ireland' through the War of Independence in *Fools of Fortune* to the contemporary Troubles in stories like 'Attracta'. Characteristically, Trevor uses the medium of fiction to dramatize individuals who are trapped in cycles of conflict, the 'battlefield continuing' through generations. As in *Mrs Eckdorf*, and so many other novels, a house has become a haven and a purposeful focus for many individuals, in the case of *Fools*, Kilneagh, the country home of a prosperous mill-owner in County Cork. Much of the house was burned down by the Black and Tans, with loss of life, including the owner, the father of Willie Quinton, a boy at this time. Willie is the central character in the novel, not only the victim of violence, but an agent of vengeful violence in turn and of suffering in the lives of many people, especially in the case of his cousin Marianne, and of their daughter, Imelda. Unaware of Marianne's pregnancy, he disappears to escape legal recourse for his murder of the former Black and Tan officer who had instigated the burning and murders at Kilneagh. For more than forty years, Marianne and her grown daughter are sheltered in the remaining part of Kilneagh, until Willie finally returns.

A few years before he comes back, Marianne reflected in her diary: 'Truncated lives, creatures of shadows. Fools of Fortune, as his father would have said; ghosts we became.'[42] By this time, 1979, most of the people directly touched by the events of the Black and Tan period in the War of Independence have died, yet two generations have absorbed degrees of suffering that have proved debilitating; they have lived 'truncated lives'. It is evident that Trevor is reflecting not only on a historical period sixty years before but on the contemporary Troubles in Northern Ireland, and his reflections broaden to all periods of civil war and destruction for the title appears to echo lines from Shakespeare's, *Henry IV*: 'thought's the slave of life, and life time's fool; / time that takes survey of all the world, / Must have a stop.'[43] *King Lear* may also be a distant echo: 'As flies to wanton boys are we to th' gods / They kill us for their sport.' The 'fools' of time, the playthings of history, appear to exist in cycles of violence that are essentially meaningless except in their power to enslave individuals; it is clear that in the lives of the individuals at Kilneagh, many other forces also enslave individuals, including a lack of courage or imagination, but the old house is a tranquil haven for all such individuals. It is what Ivy

Eckdorf in her final state of happiness imagined that O'Neill's Hotel had become.

At the end of his life, before Willie Quinton returns to Kilneagh, he reflects on the long period of time he has spent in Italy: 'Late in my life I had grown to admire the saints.... "If you study the lives of the saints," the nun in the hospital had said after Josephine had mentioned the Blessed Imelda, "you'll find that it is horror and tragedy that make them what they are. Reflecting the life of Our Lord."'[44] He is aware that his daughter has been named after the Blessed Imelda, and that she had entered a state of mental breakdown early in life as she became aware of the suffering of her mother and of the grotesque violence of her father's act of murder. He concludes that 'in Ireland it happens sometimes that the insane are taken to be saints of a kind. Legends in Ireland are born almost every day.'[45] This is a central element of storytelling that Trevor first dramatized in *Mrs Eckdorf*: the uncritical inclusion of characters who have a supernatural aura, and yet by other accounts are mad. When Willie returns to Marianne and Imelda at Kilneagh, we are told: 'Imelda is gifted, so the local people say, and bring the afflicted to her.... Her happiness is like a shroud miraculously about her, its source mysterious except to her.'[46] Like Ivy Eckdorf, she has entered a kind of 'heaven', and her parents, now reunited, feel blessed: 'They are aware that there is a miracle in this end, as remarkable as the Host which hung above the head of the child in Bologna. They are grateful for what they have been allowed, and for the mercy of their daughter's quiet world, in which there is no ugliness.'[47] This new 'legend' appears to unite in Trevor's imagination the images of Italian Catholic culture, of Renaissance painting and popular venerations, and the resources of Irish Catholic culture to create stories of supernatural powers.

The discoveries of *Mrs Eckdorf in O'Neill's Hotel* are applied here to create a contrary, religious, vision to the violences and enslavements of history. The capacity to forgive, to break the cycles of violence and suffering, is later rooted in love. *The Story of Lucy Gault*, a novel that repeats many of the elements of *Fools of Fortune*, including exile in Italy, dramatizes again over two generations the legacy of violence from the War of Independence. The experience of young love empowers Lucy Gault later in life to forgive the man who had destroyed her parents' lives; incapable of finding a role in ordinary life, he slips into a form of

madness, while she, equally unable to find a role in life, devotes herself
to visiting him in his asylum.

∾

If Trevor's early success as a novelist was due in part to his acute observation of the 'strangeness' of English society, his interest in society or
community is much less emphatic than his interest in how individuals need to find meaning or purpose in their lives. As the cast
of characters he sketches in *Mrs Eckdorf* makes clear, motivation is as
diverse as the characters themselves: the search for sexual release, or
money, love or another form of romantic inspiration, or the luck of
winning the race, escape from boredom, or simply comfort and security. The protagonist's initial motivation is revealed to be a form of
aggressive revenge for her own unhappiness, and many other characters in the novels have malevolent intentions arising from bitter childhood disillusionments. So constant is such a figure in Trevor's novels
throughout his career, in fact, that he comes close to suggesting that
evil in the world arises in circumstances of early neglect and abuse, and
this force works its way through families and communities, amounting
eventually to an impersonal malevolent force in society. *The Children
of Dynmouth* and *Felicia's Journey* are classic examples of this, but *Fools of
Fortune, The Silence in the Garden*, and *The Story of Lucy Gault* all exemplify how other motivations, such as historical injustices, can trigger
cyclical violence, the perpetration of violence taking different forms in
successive generations. In the novels, especially, such is the 'predicament that [characters] find themselves in,' and the plotlines are often
determined by the mutations of past suffering. In the case of Ivy Eckdorf,
however, she has a religious conversion, and she craves a form of personal redemption, although her wish to become an agent of goodness
in the world is unfulfilled, and her relationships with other Christian
believers, such as the porter O'Shea and Father Hennessey, are ambiguous. Each believer appears to have a different sense of how God oper-
ates in the world. What is constant is that each individual is living out
a life that is distinct and largely contingent, without any overall context of meaning or reliable sense of what is real.

   Trevor's thoughts on fictional genre and on how to represent this
vision of life arise from a sense of the fragmentation of meaning and
purpose in the modern world. His thinking centres on his own practice,
on the writing of short stories and novels and how they are distinct

fictional mediums that explore these issues in different ways. After
making clear midway through his career that he now thought of himself as primarily a writer of short stories who 'happens to write novels',
he elaborated the distinction in ways that suggest that he first thought
of himself in this way during or just after the writing of *Mrs Eckdorf*.
'I like the inkling, the shadow, of a new short story. I like the whole
business of establishing its point, for although a story need not have a
plot it must have a point.'[48] Not surprisingly, and a little reminiscent of
E. M. Forster's weariness about the necessity for plot in fiction, Trevor
prefers a visionary coherence. He speaks of the short story as 'an explosion of truth. Its strength lies in what it leaves out just as much as what
it puts in, if not more. It is concerned with the total exclusion of
meaninglessness. Life, on the other hand, is meaningless most of the
time. The novel imitates life.'[49] Impatient with the requirement to represent the 'meaninglessness' of life in a plotted novel, he refers to the
story as 'essential art'. A novel is built up like a cathedral, he says, a large
structure that is difficult to see whole, whereas a story can reveal its
coherence and meaning in the form of an 'explosion': by 'isolating an
encounter and then isolating an incident in the past you try to build
up an actual life'.[50] It is evident that Trevor does not allow himself
to think of the creation of character in a novel in this same way, for
clearly his insistence on the power of a 'glimpse' or a visionary insight
is his way of taking the reader away from the 'meaninglessness' of
life. Meaning may be found, he seems to imply, not in the public
world of his observations but in the private apprehension of order by
each individual self. In the end, he values intuition over observation,
instinctive insight over accumulated evidence. Thus, he anchors his
imagination in storytelling, a genre and a work method that allows
confident belief in something less than a 'cathedral', something that
can be seen whole.

Turning aside from English traditions of the novel, he situates his preference for the short story in an Irish tradition that reflects different cultural
circumstances. 'The Irish delight in stories, of whatever kind,' he declares
in his introduction to the *Oxford Book of Irish Short Stories*, 'because their
telling and their reception are by now instinctive.'[51] This 'mode of communication' was, to begin with, part of 'a pervasive, deeply rooted, oral
tradition', and Trevor believes that modern Irish writers inherited the
'receptive nature' of their readership. 'Portraiture thrived within its subtle-
ties,' he writes, bringing this tradition into his own practice as a storyteller;

'it withheld as much information as it released. It told as little as it dared, but often it glimpsed into a world as large and as complicated as anything either the legend or the novel could provide.'[52] Paying tribute in this way to the art and scope of the medium he embraced more and more as his primary medium in the 1970s, Trevor also gives the story and Irish Catholic culture an additional dimension of meaning: 'a willingness to believe rather than find instant virtues in scepticism'.[53] That freedom from scepticism, in addition to the orientation of his temperament and his training as a sculptor, offers him a confidence to think of himself as a storyteller working outside the conventions of the British novel.

Trevor's ideas about the short story and Irish culture are largely an echo of Frank O'Connor's approach to the short story set out in *The Lonely Voice: A Study of the Short Story* in 1963 and in his practice as a storyteller in the decades before.[54] In addition to emphasizing the historical and cultural circumstances that preserved the oral storytelling tradition, he repeats the observation that the genre 'often dealt with underdogs—what Frank O'Connor called "small men"—and increasingly as the century wore on, in hard-done-by women'.[55] Elsewhere, he elaborates: 'Heroes don't really belong in short stories. As Frank O'Connor said, "Short stories are about little people," and I agree. I find the unheroic side of people much richer and more entertaining than black and white success.'[56] Even if the examples of O'Connor and Sean O'Faoláin, two established Irish storytellers of the mid-century, influenced his own practice, and he embraced their ideas about the genre of the short story, it may be that the example of their master, Chekhov, was even more important in his practice. He is also drawn to the stories of Elizabeth Bowen—more than to her novels—and associated her with Joyce in a significant way: 'She saw the Ireland of William Carleton and Seamus O'Kelly from the same kind of distance as the one Joyce had to create for himself in order to dispel a certain claustrophobia. Synge and Yeats sought to reduce such a distance; Elizabeth Bowen simply accepted it.'[57]

The kind of 'distance' Trevor praises in Bowen's art is for him a key distinguishing feature of the writers he mentions, and in adopting it as a hallmark of his own fiction he insists that she is as Irish as any of the others. Trevor seems to be arguing against a category such as Anglo-Irish in which his work might be placed, for he wants the appropriate balance to be maintained between intimacy and distance. Implicitly, there is a crucial assertion of his Irishness here, not in political or historical or ideological declarations but in the storyteller's sensibility and tone—a cultural affiliation he claims as deeper than ancestry, sectarian affiliation, or political alignment. Just as Trevor's ideas about fictional genre reveal the emergence of a self-definition as artist, other ideas are also associated with Ireland, enabling ideas about religion, the rural landscape, and memory. These ideas were articulated in mid-career, but they refer back to an awareness that came to him as he worked on *Mrs Eckdorf in O'Neill's Hotel* and certain short stories that followed it.

He has remarked that in his early childhood, he went to convent schools, and, although he was Protestant and did not attend religious instruction, he felt no exclusion or prejudice, and, in fact, he 'liked the nuns very much'. This positive feeling about the Catholic milieu remained, and he feels alienated from Anglicanism: 'I always feel that Protestantism in England is strangely connected with the military.' In fact, these feelings appear to be associated with how he wants to view Irish life, and interestingly he sets himself apart from English Catholic novelists whom he had acknowledged as mentors earlier; 'English writers like Graham Greene, for instance, and Evelyn Waugh, became Catholics because they were frustrated. But Ireland being a religious country, the religious side of people is satisfied more naturally than it is in England.'[58] He has no interest in becoming a Catholic, although he does think his books 'are religious' in some broad sense which he characterizes as 'a kind of primitive belief in God' given to many characters. It appears that he grounds this 'primitive belief' in the country that is 'more naturally religious'—more hospitable to a sense of the miraculous and the mysterious, he seems to imply—and so Mrs Eckdorf in her religious quest is brought to Ireland and, as a Protestant outsider to the culture, appears to undergo a conversion to this 'primitive' or 'natural' religion. Of necessity, its origins and its effects are shown to operate in essentially mysterious ways and remain open to multiple interpretations.

Given the opportunity to prepare a book on Irish writing, Trevor chose the theme of landscape, although he is quick to say it is only 'a writer's journey, a tour of places which other writers have felt affection for also, or have known excitement or alarm in'.[59] The book is characteristically evasive, largely given over to photographs and lengthy quotations from writers of previous centuries, with predictable linking commentary. He implies that he is present in the book because he is like these other Irish writers who have felt affection for these places.

Elsewhere, in *Excursions*, he comments: 'it is affection ...that causes you to want to know what you never will.'[60] His choice of 'landscape in literature' for this book and his emphasis on 'affection' for place as inspirational indicate that the realistic writer, a disciple of Joyce, must also be considered a Romantic. This last sentence surely echoes Keats's 'I am certain of nothing but of the holiness of the Heart's affections and the truth of Imagination.' Reminiscent too of Keats is Trevor's' ability to disappear into his characters and his work, his embrace of 'negative capability' which has given to his style what John Banville has admired as 'systematic self-effacement'.

The move away from English material and the return to Ireland allowed this 'affection' for place and the 'ambiguous voice' to emerge as the true voice of the fiction. It might be that Trevor's comments on Beckett may clarify this change in his own work best, for in an essay in *Excursions* he focuses on the decisive moment when Beckett discovered the definitive direction for his work. It is a moment when Beckett freed himself from a deliberate search for philosophical meanings and set the course for discovering in practice his writing self: 'His intellectualism and severity had blocked from him the simple fact that his own introspections constituted the roots of the art he sought to express. Real people and real places got him going.... His memory, and what he does with it, is what matters.'[61] The work of Beckett and of Trevor may appear to have little in common, but this statement surely hints at an identification that goes beyond his admiration of Beckett's reclusive temperament and his silence about the provenance or meaning of his work. The essay's assertion that the most abstract quality of Beckett's work is a distraction from its 'roots' in 'real places and real people' and in 'memory' might suggest that they are opposites, but clearly Trevor feels a deep kinship with him, a particular affection that becomes evident as he distances himself from Wilde, Yeats, and even Joyce. While he understands the enabling 'outward show' which all three writers invented to dramatize the artistic self, he knows that all of them in the end concentrated on 'the practical writing of the lines' and that the 'inspiration' or the public persona is of much less importance.

What Trevor says of characterization in his fiction seems to have a reference also to himself:

[Time] both heals and destroys, depending on the nature of the wound; it reveals the character. There is either bitterness or recovery: neither can take place without time. Time is the most interesting thing to write about besides people—everything I write has to do with it.... Memory also forms character—the way you remember things makes you who you are.[62]

Trevor's comments on Beckett suggest that in his own case, behind his self-effacing persona, he 'instinctively' knew what Beckett had to learn, that the 'unique nature' of the writer's 'human apparatus' is grounded in personal memory. It may be that Trevor is closer to Beckett than he admits, that what he calls Beckett's 'block' attributable to 'intellectualism and severity', may have been something he knew personally for other reasons and that in his return to Ireland in imagination and memory, he too freed himself from a 'block'. He became capable of writing of 'Catholic Ireland' and of drawing on his own past.

∼

Trevor's transformation may be clarified further by placing *Mrs Eckdorf* next to the short story 'The Ballroom of Romance', written soon after the novel. The stories of the two women protagonists, Ivy Eckdorf and Bridie, contrast in so many ways that placing them side by side might seem pointless, but they are two aspects of the same effort to reorient himself and to refine a new 'Irish' style. If *Mrs Eckdorf* attempts to deepen everything Trevor had learned about fiction-writing through the work of the 1960s, and, perhaps, to articulate a critical relationship to that body of work, 'The Ballroom of Romance' may be seen as a work pointing forward in his career and exemplifying his deliberate re-rooting in another tradition of storytelling. *Mrs Eckdorf* is a kind of clearing of the decks so that, a 'block' removed, he is free to write a new kind of story.

In striking contrast to all Trevor's earlier fictions, including *Mrs Eckdorf*, 'The Ballroom of Romance' is set in the countryside, focuses on a single character, and uses a point of view that is sympathetically close to the central character and yet also restrained and ambiguous in its effect. It seems to exemplify everything Trevor said later about the genre as a glimpse, a portrait, an incident, 'the lonely voice'. Bridie, the protagonist, has given the best years of her life to caring for her invalided father on an isolated farm. She assumed the role in adolescence when her mother died, and although her father still calls her 'girl', twenty years have gone by. When her father remarks 'It's a terrible thing for you, girl', she responds 'Amn't I as happy here as anywhere?', 'but her father knew she was pretending and was saddened because the weight of circumstances had so harshly interfered with her life'.[63] As if to prepare the reader for the depth of ambiguity in this communication between father and daughter, the conflicted thoughts of Bridie when she compares her adult life with her fellow classmates in town have been revealed:

Most of them had families of their own by now. 'You're lucky to be peaceful in the hills,' they said to Bridie, 'instead of stuck in a hole like this.'... As she cycled back to the hills on a Friday Bridie often felt that they truly envied her her life, and she found it surprising that they should do so. If it hadn't been for her father she'd have wanted to work in the town also.[64]

What kind of happiness is possible for Bridie in the 'peaceful' hills? the story prompts us to ask. Would she truly be happier in the town? Is there some way she can be less isolated and alone than she is with her father?

The answers to such questions hover over her weekly visits to the Ballroom of Romance. She cycles unaccompanied across the hills, 'but she did not mind the journey'. In spite of its name, this is a place of low expectations. 'The dance-hall, owned by Mr Justin Dwyer, was miles from anywhere, a lone building by the roadside with treeless boglands all around and a gravel expanse in front of it.'[65] The façade of the building is pink, and there are coloured lights. Trevor's even tone throughout mingles details of how Mr Dwyer conducts his successful business, as he has done for decades, and details of the meeting and parting on the dance-floor of ageing men and women, who have known each other's hopes and evasions for decades. In a grim charade of 'romance', they dance and part, conversation an exchange of familiar clichés, their calculations and desires traced by inadvertent revelations.

When Bridie enters, the Romantic Jazz Band 'was playing a familiar melody of the past, "The Destiny Waltz"'. The three amateur musicians, all middle-aged men, drive out from the town each week, and Bridie has formed a friendly attachment to the drummer, Dano Ryan, and has mild hopes of marrying him. On her way to the cloakroom, he greets her: 'He was idle for a moment with his drums, "The Destiny Waltz" not calling for much attention from him.'[66] This is the kind of masterful sentence that illustrates the new style of Trevor, its apparently casual details, simply etching in a background or a context that sets the scene, yet, already knowing Bridie's dilemma, the reader feels that this is an evening on which her destiny may be decided irrevocably. If the music does not call 'for much attention from him', Dano is also indifferent to Bridie's heightened expectations, or pretends to be as he keeps conversation at a safe distance from any hint of more than routine interest in her life. In the course of this evening, as she and the other women dance with possibly eligible but really unworthy marriage partners, Bridie recalls how over the years she has considered all of them in passing, and now remembers her one brief attachment to a young man, her only experience of love, although he left her and emigrated to Wolverhampton. Her last candidate for a husband is Dano Ryan, and, of course, on this evening, she discovers 'instinctively' that he will marry a widow with whom he is boarding in town.

She discovers that her destiny is to be alone, and realizes that in any case she did not really love this man. It would be a life of habitual pretence. She reflects again on 'the weight of circumstances' that had trapped her with her father and knows that the only choices available to her were to be with him and to stand hopefully 'in a wayside ballroom'.[67] Now she knows that this part of her life is over, she will never return to the ballroom, and she is inclined to weep, yet she continues to make light conversation with Dano Ryan 'as though nothing had happened'. 'Her father had more right to weep, having lost a leg. He suffered in a greater way, yet he remained kind and concerned for her.'[68] She cycles away, accompanied for a time by Bowser Egan, a drunk bachelor whom she may well end up marrying after her father dies. He will take advantage of her and yet she is not sure she can live alone. 'She rode through the night as on Saturday nights for years she had ridden and never would ride again because she'd reached a certain age.'[69] Time determines everything in this narrow world with few choices, perhaps none, and she appears to face a future devoid of hope of 'romance'; the story appears to posit a life in which personal freedom and happiness are surrendered to 'circumstances'— the 'predicament' in which Trevor says he places his characters—and the main challenge is to adapt to what will inevitably happen.

An extraordinary feature of this grimly predestined world, reminiscent of Hardy's, is that Bridie appears to have no religious belief. She attends Mass, we are told, but her self-sacrifice is not orchestrated as a search for personal redemption; this marks a striking contrast with *Mrs Eckdorf in O'Neill's Hotel*. From this story on, Trevor seems to have accepted more and more that this landscape of 'bleak splendour' is the counter world to the false glamour and deceptions of middle-class urban London and to the desperate fantasies and malevolence of his working-class characters. Within this Irish world that he had known and now returns to with acute insight, he finds an almost Beckettian vision of the narrow boundaries of destiny. Thirty years after he wrote 'The Ballroom of Romance', Trevor returned to write a new version with a male protagonist. When the young man's father dies on a small isolated farm, he decides to return to live with his mother. 'The Hill Bachelors' ends: 'Guilt was misplaced, goodness hardly came into it. Her widowing and the mood of a capricious time were not of consequence, no more than a flicker in a scheme of things that had always been there. Enduring, unchanging, the hills had waited for him, claiming one of their own.'[70]

'The Ballroom of Romance' is the first in a long line of stories that move away from the carefully etched urban and contemporary setting and from social drama into a characteristic treatment of an individual's experience of time and acceptance of an incomplete life. Memories and dreams deepen the sense of a life lived in the continuum of the past and the future, but the inner life of the single character is the site of hard-found adjustments to an immutable ordinariness. The delicate balance of madness and sainthood which William Trevor explored so extravagantly in the high drama of *Mrs Eckdorf* is now replaced by a style of subtle indirection in which the silence of his protagonists protects their reasoning and their rawest feelings from public display. The effect is simultaneously one of heart-breaking sadness and melancholic endurance and also an allegorical resonance that suggests eternal truths of how humans must always live with 'the weight of circumstances'. While the facts of the observed life and the impoverished rural community would lead one to feel the imprisonment and destruction of the individual's spirit, the even narrative voice seems to honour the self-sacrifice and the clear recognition of the limits of what is possible.

∾

Although the date 1971 is given in 'The Ballroom of Romance' as the year in which the main action takes place, the old-fashioned world of ballrooms and bicycles that Bridie inhabits appears to be metaphorical rather than sociological. The enclosed local world in which she moves has an aura of an earlier time, the world of her parents, perhaps, in which she passed her childhood, or even going further back. In other words, the story appears to arise less from Trevor's observation of rural Ireland of 1971 than from his own memories which were embedded in the 1930s and 1940s. And if his memories inform him as he writes—'A huge amount of what I write about is internal, a drifting back into childhood'[71]—his childhood world was to a great extent the world of his family, especially given that they moved to so many different towns during those years. While he remembers those towns vividly, he also recalls displacement and a sense of homelessness in his own experience and in that of his mother. That pattern will be continued in his own adult experience for many years after graduating and then emigrating to England, until he settled in middle age in rural Devon and then began work on *Mrs Eckdorf*. His Irish work is deeply rooted in an earlier time, and in the lives of his parents and the towns they lived in. *Mrs Eckdorf in O'Neill's Hotel* and 'The Ballroom of Romance' appear to have re-rooted his imagination in the world of memory and in a vision of what remains constant in the human condition. Even a novel such as *Love and Summer*, written forty years later, continues to share the vision of 'The Ballroom of Romance' or, for instance, *Reading Turgenev*, written midway between these two fictions.

While individuals live in historical time and in specific geographical places, a sense of the supernatural or the eternal may enter into individual consciousness or inform actions that are determined less by belief or romantic fulfilment than by endurance. The closing essay in *Excursions* touches on these matters briefly when Trevor writes about one of his favourite hill walks in Ireland, an off-the-beaten-track place without any historical or mythological connections so that it makes no claim to represent 'the elusive spirit of Ireland' as other celebrated places do.

Nature is defiant on Europe's western rock, and you would swear that this Ireland all around you has never been different. It is the only wisp of romance you are offered as you tramp on, up to the next small lake. It's a personal attachment, of course: your own place.... The secret of beauty may be here, and probably is, but it isn't yours to discover.[72]

The individual's roots in a local place of origin, Trevor seems to argue, connect him to a certainty and a sense of stability, something 'that has never been different'. It is an assertion of his Irishness that transcends sect or history, an imaginative vision of an anchoring of self that underlies all the fictions of uncertainty and change. It is this vision that is embodied in 'The Ballroom of Romance' and it offers a contrast to the 'meaninglessness' of abused and suffering lives as represented in *Mrs Eckdorf in O'Neill's Hotel* and other novels.

Another essay in that collection may also offer insight into the enigmatic tone of Bridie's self-sacrificing endurance. 'Fields of Battle' describes Trevor's parents' marriage as a battle drawn out over forty years.

> They were victims of their innocence when chance threw them together and passion beguiled them, leaving them to live with a mistake and to watch their field of battle expanding with each day that passed. They gave their love to their children and were loved in return, fiercely, unwaveringly. But not for a moment could that heal the wounds they carried to their graves.[73]

Trevor writes brilliantly and briefly of what it felt like to live in his home, and he greatly admires the honesty of his parents in not pretending something they did not feel, in enduring. Elsewhere, and more than once, he dismisses the idea that his 'sense of tragedy' may come from the Troubles and from Irish history and says it comes from his childhood. He did not write this essay until 1992, but two decades before, while his parents were still alive, he had returned to the Irish material he may not have wanted to examine explicitly: memories of lovelessness and homelessness. It is this personal inheritance embedded in memory that charged the vision and voice of those fictions.[74]

4

Mavis Gallant's *Green Water, Green Sky*

'Authentic hallucinations'

Apart from a few stories published in small literary reviews in Montreal, Mavis Gallant's long career began with the publication of a story in the *New Yorker* in September 1951.[1] Over five decades, the magazine published more than a hundred of her stories, while a small number of longer fictions appeared elsewhere, some only accompanying short fiction in volume publication, and two, *Green Water, Green Sky* and *A Fairly Good Time*, on their own. Gallant referred to such longer fictions variously as 'a novella', 'a short novel', or 'a novel', even in the case of *Green Water, Green Sky*, a 'novel' published in 1959, although it consists of four interconnected fictions, three of which had appeared separately in the *New Yorker*. The first story of Flor McCarthy, 'Green Water, Green Sky', was published in June 1959. It was followed a month later by 'Travellers Must Be Content', and in August 1959 by 'August', a publishing schedule that suggests that they were written together, and probably at least a year earlier.[2] One of her critics has described *Green Water, Green Sky* as 'a pivotal work in Gallant's canon' which marks her movement away from the more conventional short stories of her first decade.[3]

Gallant's body of fiction is not simply a long sequence of separate stories published in the *New Yorker* with some evident repetitions and interconnections; rather, *Green Water, Green Sky* marks the definitive beginning of a career as a constantly experimental writer in prose. Working in a broad tradition of realism and representation, she used her fiction as a narrative means of observing certain conditions in various cultural groups—Parisians, North American exiles in Europe, post-war Germans, Montrealers (English- and French-speaking)—but her experiments with narrative voice, fluid point of view, time, memory, and dream are integral to her investigative style. That style emerged in *Green Water, Green Sky*, and it is inseparable from her concern with identity, thought of in terms of voice, what she will later refer to as the 'authentic voice' of the dead.[4]

Mavis Gallant (née Young) was born in Montreal in 1922 of an English-born father and an American mother, both of Protestant background.[5] Beginning at the age of four, and for a number of years, she was sent as a boarder to a Catholic, entirely French-speaking convent, where, as she noted much later, she had her first experience of being a 'foreigner'. 'It was a singular thing [for her parents] to do', Gallant has written, 'and in those days unheard of. It left me with two systems of behavior, divided by syntax and tradition; two environments to consider, one becalmed in a long twilight of nineteenth-century religiosity; two codes of social behavior; much practical experience of the difference between a rule and a moral point.' Gallant suggests here that her identity as a writer is anchored in her personal experience of displacement at a very young age, in her awareness of contrasting cultural perspectives, and, most of all, in a self-conscious relationship with two languages. 'Somewhere in this duality may be the exact point of the beginning of writing',[6] she concludes.

The child soon became fluent in French, and although she later attended English-speaking schools—a great number of different schools in both Canada and the United States—Gallant would spend most of her adult life in Paris, living in a French-speaking milieu. She did not write in French, however, and more than once she insisted on an important distinction:

I owe it to children's books—picture books, storybooks, the English and American classics—that I absorbed once and for all the rhythm of English prose, the order of words in an English sentence and how they are spelled.... Nothing supposed, daydreamed, created, or invented would enter my mind by way of French.... for stories and storytelling there was only one sound.'[7]

This fable of childhood and writing appears to be embedded in the idea of preserving her autonomy and independence in a 'foreign' environment, and in its earliest phase, the convent school years, the sound and rhythms of English preserved that 'language of the imagination'.

Gallant's family life in Montreal collapsed when she was ten. Her father disappeared. She was told he had gone back to England on a visit, and it was only at age thirteen that she discovered that he had actually died, in circumstances that were not explained. 'In many many of the things I write, someone has vanished', she said in an interview, although she rarely spoke of her work or noted its characteristics, 'And it's often the father. And there is often the sense that nothing is very safe.'[8] She noted that many people found a physical resemblance with him when she became adult, and in her twenties the image of his failure became a spur to her ambition: her father aspired to be a painter, and many people thought of him as an artist, but he had failed to achieve anything at the time of his death soon after age thirty. One of her first stories in the *New Yorker*, 'Wing's Chips', is about a young girl's observation of her father, a painter, who is outside both English and French communities and has won little respect from anyone. Gallant said many times that she was determined at an early age not to repeat the pattern of her father's life, and so at age twenty-eight she left her secure employment in Montreal to become a full-time writer in Europe.

In the next decade, she settled for periods in cities in many different countries, France, Spain, Austria and Italy, among them, and then in Menton on the Côte d'Azur, before, in 1960, taking up permanent residence in Paris. Before she left Montreal, she knew that a story would be published in the *New Yorker*, 'Madeline's Birthday', and the regular publication of her stories in the magazine through her first decade in Europe, and in the following decades, allowed her to have an independent life as a writer. At first it seems that she was determined to investigate a variety of European cultures, and stories of the 1950s are set in various countries, often depicting migrant characters, American expatriates and others. *Green Water, Green Sky* may, at first glance, appear to be merely such a story, with its settings in Venice, Paris, and Provence, but in fact it is an investigation of the nature of storytelling itself, of narrative reliability, subjectivity, and memory. In the portrait of the central character, Flor McCarthy, she depicts a young woman who fails to become an independent adult, but the narrator's compassionate distance is characteristic of an oblique kind of autobiographical narrative. This fiction is a portrait of the artist that clarified the ways in which her development had to be grounded not only in the acute observation of European culture but in her own personal experience of impermanence and hallucination.

In spite of her residence in Canada and the United States until late 1950, Gallant's artistic and intellectual interests were primarily oriented towards European cultures. She remarked that this was something she had inherited from her parents, both of whom had recent family links to Europe, and in the somewhat bohemian ambience of her childhood and early adulthood in Montreal she was exposed to modern trends in European painting and to classical music (her parents played cello and violin, her grandmother the piano) in addition to literature. Apart from classical Russian and French novelists of the nineteenth century, whose work she immersed herself in at a young age, her main interest was modernism, and, specifically, in fiction, Virginia Woolf and Katherine Mansfield. 'I admired her enormously', Gallant said of Mansfield, referring to her earliest years of writing short stories, although in later decades, it seems that Mansfield's mentor, Anton Chekhov, and Marcel Proust became the writers Gallant reread most constantly.

Yet if these established writers were of deep interest to her, the late 1930s and then the wartime years were her formative decade. Her 'first political experience [was] the Spanish Civil War. . . . I was fascinated from the moment the announcement came on the radio. I was nearly fourteen, and this always haunted me.'[9] She became a passionate anti-fascist, a Marxist, and a key book was Lenin and Zinoviev's *Against the Stream*. Her interest in politics and in an historical understanding of political and cultural convictions lie behind, for instance, her sustained experiment in using fiction to understand the German lower-middle class, the culture in which Nazism prospered; the work she devoted to the case of Gabrielle Roussier in France; her interest in the Dreyfus case; and, towards the end of her life, her arrangement of her *Selected Stories*, not chronologically, according to composition or publication, but as a way of reading 'The Thirties and Forties', 'The Fifties', 'The Sixties', and so on. Her political convictions are never overtly expressed in her fiction, but the satirical energies, the acute detection of prejudices, the insistence on judgement of certain kinds of behaviour, are integral to the textures of her narratives. In *Home Truths: Selected Canadian Stories* she includes as an epigraph a sentence from Boris Pasternak which is surely definitive of her own position: 'Only personal independence matters'. Her experimental stories work within and against the grain of historical investigation, but her method is far from naturalism, reportage, documentation, or polemics.

When her family disintegrated, she was left in the care of a number of guardians in various places in Canada and the United States and eventually close to New York City in her teenage years. She spoke a number of times about the city as a place where she discovered pleasure and the freedom to laugh—she meant this as a marker of contrast with the puritanical and repressed homes she had lived in previously. In the cinema, in New York, people laughed spontaneously, a sign of freedom she welcomed, but perhaps more important was the influence of her guardians at this time: one a Freudian psychoanalyst who had actually been analysed by Freud. Neil Besner reports that 'at one point in her life she "went through a great period of Freud" and that his ideas were "gospel" to her, "almost like a code"'.[10] New York seems to represent to her a place without inhibition in which personal independence might be encouraged. Her mother had remarried a man she had fallen in love with before the father's disappearance (something the young Gallant appears to have known intuitively). By the age of fifteen, she had chosen to have no further contact with her mother, and three years later, she returned alone to Montreal, bringing with her books by Lenin and others which she had assumed would be unavailable in Catholic Quebec. She sketches her youthful self some years after settling back in Montreal: 'Imagine being twenty-two, being the intensely left-wing political romantic I was, passionately anti-fascist, having believed that a new kind of civilization was going to grow out of the ruins of war—out of the victory over fascism.'[11] Literature appears to have been more deeply rooted than political activism, however, and she never ceased her story-writing in these years or gave up her ambition to be a writer.

As an aspiring writer and a woman for whom personal independence mattered more than anything, Mavis Gallant paid careful attention to women writers who came to maturity in those years, such as Eudora Welty and Sylvia Townsend-Warner. More than the others, one writer, who had already absorbed the modernism of Woolf and Mansfield, appears to have drawn her attention in intimate ways. This was Elizabeth Bowen. Gallant rarely wrote reviews or public comments on other writers, but in a review of a biography of Bowen, she wrote: 'For a certain generation Elizabeth Bowen was not merely a writer, but part of the bridge one begins to cross at about 13, when fiction and life are still magically fused and books contain an element of prophecy.'[12] Gallant suggests that Bowen provided a vision that helped her to grow towards adulthood, but the reference to 'prophecy' has the weight of a retrospective sense of how Bowen was central to the emergence of a writing self. More than this, the reference to a specific age, when 'fiction and life are still magically fused', is significant because, as in Bowen's case, very many of Gallant's earliest fictions, including *Green Water, Green Sky*, focus on girls becoming young women, often with absent or dependent mothers. Both are frequently drawn to the emotionally charged experiences and insights of children and acknowledge that the writing self incorporates something of the unique vulnerability and imaginative suspension of disbelief of that age. Beginning in the late 1920s and through the 1930s, Bowen wrote a series of novels of young women searching for an authentic life, much as Gallant herself did in a less conventional narrative style, two decades later, but the identification in Gallant's mind is clear: 'Readers who once drew on *The Death of the Heart* and *To the North* as part of their own experience' is surely an autobiographical statement. Later, speaking of a writer's presence in her style, she remarked of Bowen: 'The fact is that she does not stand cutting, that no one sentence gives a hint of the underlying flame. The bonfire is *all The House in Paris*, *all* 'Mysterious Kor.' On another occasion, Gallant referred to the former as a 'great novel', and the latter as 'that pure and perfect story': 'I knew it almost by heart. It's one of her wartime London stories. I loved her stories.'[13]

The two writers focused with special intensity on the fate of young women, especially orphaned, bereaved, or abandoned girls, and such personal circumstances in both cases seem to be the 'bridge' between life and books, but the historical circumstances of the time fused with personal experience to give Bowen's wartime fiction an especial interest for Gallant. *The Heat of the Day* reached a very wide audience, and her volume of stories, *The Demon Lover*, also reflected the 'lucid abnormality' of the time. Bowen wrote an Afterword for the volume of stories when it appeared in 1945, and many statements there about her wartime art are echoed in later remarks of Gallant and indeed in *Green Water, Green Sky*. 'I do not say that these stories wrote themselves— aesthetically or intellectually speaking, I found the writing of them very difficult', Bowen says,

but I was never in a moment's doubt as to *what* I was to write. . . . The acts in them had an authority which I could not question. . . . They were sparks from experience, an experience not necessarily my own.... It seems to me that during the war the overcharged subconsciousness of everybody overflowed and merged.'[14]

Gallant's account of the genesis of stories parallels this, and her phrase on the 'underlying flame' of style is surely an echo. Bowen speaks of the stories as a form of 'resistance writing', and rereading them, finds in the book 'a rising tide of hallucination.... The hallucinations are an unconscious, instinctive, saving resort on the part of the characters.' Bowen and Gallant also are insistent on registering the layers of reality and unreality that envelop people and places, physical objects and states of mind.

'The first flash of fiction arrives without words', Gallant wrote in the Preface to her *Selected Stories*.

It consists of a fixed image, like a slide, or (closer still) a freeze frame, showing characters in a simple situation.... The quick arrival and departure of the silent image can be likened to the first moments of a play, before anything is said. The difference is that the characters in the frame are not seen, but envisioned, and do not have to speak to be explained.[15]

She continues to outline the compositional process, but it is evident that these silent visual images are the basis of the 'hallucinations' she speaks of in *Green Water, Green Sky*, and while she uses highly elaborated speaking voices in her third-person and first-person narrators, this combination of enquiring voice and haunting image is the foundation of her mature style. This book brings such dreamlike images to life in a set of stories that deny narrative expectations and novelistic outcomes; it is also a kind of manifesto and an oblique story of the making of an artist.

Green Water, Green Sky is a work that reveals a mature artist emerging from the apprenticeships of story-writing during the 1940s and 1950s and of her work as a journalist on the *Montreal Standard* for six years. In Montreal, she succeeded in becoming independent. She married, and divorced, and as a journalist, she wrote features, many of them about French-speaking and working class *Québécois*, reviewed radio programmes and conducted interviews, often with artists; in general, she had great freedom to initiate her own topics and follow her own interests. Yet by 1950 she was ready to leave behind such journalistic genres and go to Europe to concentrate exclusively on the writing of fiction. It took almost a decade of travelling through post-war Europe and writing stories to find her 'true voice'.

The indistinct portrait of Flor McCarthy, a young American drifting around Europe with her mother in the post-war years and, then, also with her husband, is at the heart of these four fictions, and yet in only one of them does the narrator present in close-up this young woman struggling to gain personal independence.[16] Elsewhere, the reader becomes aware of her presence indirectly, as she is seen by those who are closest to her, her mother, Bonnie, her young cousin, George, her husband, Bob, and by a friend of her mother, Wishart. The omniscient narrator situates the perspectives of all these characters and their various partial views, and a more explanatory view of Flor and of those about her is provided by patterns of mirroring, recollection, and embedded symbols and motifs.[17] This 'novel' focuses on an investigation of a young woman who loses her 'voice', her identity, and does not really survive, but the fiction itself is a triumphant discovery of a personal writing voice and of the confident independence it embodies.

Part I, originally the story '*Green Water, Green Sky*', is centrally focused on George Fairlee, aged seven, at first, and then aged seventeen. In both scenes, he is associated with his cousin Flor, first in Venice and then in New York, soon after her wedding to Bob Harris. There have been other brief meetings of the two cousins during the intervening years, we are told in summary, but George is not mentioned again until Part IV, when he is again the central character, now aged nineteen and spending an evening in Paris with his Aunt Bonnie and Bob Harris. Memories from the first meeting in Venice return, as he tries to orient himself on this first European journey alone, but essentially, on this evening, he discovers his own independence by observing the responses of the others to Flor's breakdown. By distancing himself from Bonnie, Bob, and Flor herself, and their Parisian world, he also provides the reader with an insight into Flor's condition and this expatriate, somewhat Jamesian, world. In this sense, the 'novel' is framed by the presence of George, and is given thematic coherence. More than this, Gallant's narrator allows the reader to obliquely follow his thought process from childhood to manhood in such a way that the vision and aesthetic principles guiding Gallant's work are sketched.

In Parts II and III, when George is not present—the summer in Paris of Flor's breakdown and the summer in Cannes two years earlier when Flor meets Bob—the reader is introduced directly to Bonnie and to Bob. Gallant's sketch of Bonnie is deft and devastating, first a

visual image of her trying on a hat: 'She pulled it on her head, tugging
with both hands. The frown, the pout, the obstinate gestures, were
those of a child. It was a deliberate performance, and new: after years
of struggling to remain adult in a grown-up world, she had found it
unrewarding.'[18] She had been divorced by her husband over a dozen
years before, and is now fifty-two, 'a classic, middle-aged charmer', but
aside from the social roles she plays, she has became 'a lost, sallow,
frightened Bonnie, wandering from city to city in Europe, clutching
her daughter by the hand'.[19] Living in a large apartment with servants,
this desperate woman has become grotesquely self-serving, now dom-
inating and controlling Bob for financial gain, as she has dominated
Flor for psychological gain.

In Part II, Flor is far advanced in her withdrawal from her mother
and her husband—the two of them, in spite of mutual dislike, thrown
together—and Bob is introduced as a pragmatic businessman at sea in
his relationship with Flor: 'too much had been taken away in his wife's
retreat and he had been, without knowing it, building on what was left:
money and his own charm'. Yet Flor has moments of tenderness
towards him:

She looked at her husband and saw that whatever protected him had left him
at that moment; he seemed pitiable and without confidence. She might have
said, Forgive me, or even, Help me, and it might have been different between
them, if not better, but Bonnie came in ... and past love, that delicate goblet,
was shattered on the spot.[20]

In addition, in Part II, a peripheral character is introduced, who is to a
degree in Flor's situation, and the contrast is instructive. Doris, a young
American who lives in Flor's apartment building, is now adrift since
her husband has left her and moved to Rome. She is alone and desperate, but she realizes that 'the solution for me was a decision and now
I am going home. I am not going *away* but going *home*.' Even if her
decision is a retreat to a past life, it is implied that this expatriate has a
will to act on her own behalf, something that Bonnie has not allowed
Flor to develop.

Part III is largely an account of a summertime visit by Bonnie's friend
Wishart, a transatlantic poseur, an English squire when in America, an
American when in Europe. Gallant's satirical rapier is at its sharpest in
depicting the well-named Wishart: 'he moved in a gassy atmosphere of
goodwill and feigned successes. He seemed invulnerable. Strangers

meeting him for the first time often thought he must be celebrated, and wondered why they had never heard of him before.'[21] In the foreground, the fantasy of Bonnie and Wishart is played out, both of them observing the relationship of Flor and Bob develop. In a panic, Bonnie has the idea that Wishart might marry Flor, a grotesque and wholly egocentric idea which leads to Wishart's precipitate departure. The young couple are actually falling in love in a way that is beyond the capacity of either Bonnie or Wishart: 'She thought that what she felt now came because of the passage of light: it was a concrete sensation of happiness, as if happiness could be felt, lifted, carried around. She had not experienced anything of the kind before.'[22] The feeling is mutual: 'He remembered her long hair, the wrinkled sheets, the blanket thrown back because of the heat. It was the prophetic instant, the compression of feeling that occurs in childhood and in dreams.'[23] Yet the independence Flor and Bob achieve in that summer in Cannes is eroded, and it is clear that their inability to free themselves from the controlling presence of Bonnie has led to the terminal point already seen close-up in Part II.

In chronological terms, Part IV is then a continuation of Part II, but in narrative terms it is George's development that is foregrounded, and the circumstances he finds in Paris are the occasion for him to draw certain conclusions about his aunt and her role in Flor's life, which the narrator has already revealed.

Nothing had prepared him for this situation, in which he kept trying to find his feet. 'George is so lucky,' his mother had once said. 'He's had all the good disadvantages.' His training was planned for the social rather than the human collapse. His shed youth now seemed a piling up of hallucinations, things heard and seen that were untrue or of no use to him.[24]

He has grown up in the WASP Fairlee family in which controlled, 'respectable', behaviour could be accommodated, but this training was not a preparation for the 'human collapse' of Flor and those about her. He realizes that Flor was not prepared for it either, and her mother's social expertise—although she was not a Fairlee by birth and formation—was also inadequate. Essentially, George must quickly find some first principles in this world of flux and anguish, and the often satirical perspective of the narrative shifts to a sympathetic view of a young man whose perceptions are grounded on an aesthetic and moral basis. This concluding sequence offers indirectly an understanding of how George and Flor complement each other and also an understanding of

Gallant's own guiding principles. George's quest—and the narrator's—
is for a proper way to imagine the lost Flor.

The 'novel' is not structured by time but by displacement and, in
terms of fictional realism, by incoherence; the narrative emphasis falls
on intensely realized brief scenes, some theatrical, some dreamlike,
linked by an omniscient narrative voice. The reader is challenged to
find coherence by observing patterns, parallels, mirrorings, echoes,
chiaroscuro effects, to find order and purpose in a fiction that denies
the coherence of psychological or social realism. In effect, the reader is
placed in a situation of disorientation that resembles that of Flor and
George. Gallant's aesthetic means are anchored not in plot or character
but in voice and heightened visual scenes, 'hallucinations'.[25]

These settings and events may recall some of the work of Henry James,
Edith Wharton, or F. Scott Fitzgerald as a later study of well-off Americans
adrift in Europe in the decade immediately after the end of the Second
World War. The epigraph, taken from *As You Like It*, '…when I was at
home, I / was in a better place, but / travellers must be content', reinforces
the idea that exile and displacement are its subjects, and in general this is
so, yet the title lends another emphasis to its thematic preoccupations.
The tension in the compressed style, its reliance on highly charged
brief scenes, the rejection of chronology and conventional realism
for an allusive, dreamlike, narrative all focus the reader's attention on
Gallant's distinctive style and on the nature of Flor's alienation.

From the first paragraph, Gallant establishes that these exotic or
romantic settings are places of disillusionment and, indeed, squalor and
desolation. *The Other Paris*, Gallant's earlier book of stories, published
in 1956, had introduced readers to her typical deflation of the dreams
of tourists and travellers, and their attempts to discover how to 'be
content'. Here the narrator is close to the consciousness of George,
and his observation of the gondolas on the Grand Canal sets the tone:

> If he had been given something the right length, a broom, say, he could have
> stirred the hardly moving layer of morning muck, the orange halves, the pulpy
> melons, the rotting bits of lettuce, black under water, green above. Water
> lapped against the gondolas moored below the terrace. He remembered the
> sound, the soft, dull slapping, all his life.[26]

That sound is memorable, not for any gratuitous naturalism but
because this is the site of a 'betrayal' that remains definitive. Without

warning or explanation, his parents abandoned him for a day to the company of Bonnie and Flor.[27] While George's experience marked him, Bonnie considers his distress 'selfish', and regards him as a spoiled child, but in fact, his parents accept that they made a mistake in introducing him to the feeling of abandonment, and try to make up for this: 'After that day in Venice they had sworn they would never leave him again, never, ever, and they had kept their word, so that their love for him was a structure, and he was inside it.'[28] By the end of Part I, he is grown and about to leave them for college, and in this and other ways, the narrator suggests that this 'structure' was, perhaps, as much a prison and a false enclosure as a protective one. In spite of these later, protected years, the 'betrayal' is an unforgettable and educational fact of life that allows him to grasp intuitively the nature of Flor's inner life, shaped as it is by abandonment and then homelessness.

Venice, Cannes, and Paris may be desirable places for affluent Americans to stop, but, in fact, Flor is searching for 'a home for the homeless', and for a short time she falls in love with Bob Harris. They become lovers, and she is happy: 'Lacking an emotional country, it might be possible to consider another person one's home. She pressed her face against his unmoving arm, accepting everything imperfect, as one accepts a faulty but beloved country, or the language in which one's thoughts are formed.'[29] Harris is also an American, in Paris to manage his father's business of wine importing, but in theory he is more definitively homeless than Flor, since he has no past, in the sense of American ancestry and traditions. His father escaped from the Warsaw ghetto. Bonnie has an artificial and snobbish sense of the Fairlie family traditions, from which she is now geographically estranged owing to her divorce. The narrator seems to suggest that the past is indeed another country, and that whatever Bob Harris's limitations, the circumstances of his father's exile have a reality that made it necessary to establish his personal identity without benefit of family or tradition. It is not suggested that Bob Harris is in any way anchored by a Jewish tradition or identity, other than, perhaps, business, although he fails to understand why Flor does not return to America, if it is the 'home' she has lost. The narrator makes clear, however, that more important than a home country is 'the language in which one's thoughts are formed'.

A key conversation between Flor and Bob reveals that her sense of alienation and lost identity is represented by the inauthenticity of the speaking voice. She is trying to convey to him that she is governed by an irrational fear: 'He looked at her curiously, for she had used a false voice; not as Bonnie sometimes did, but as if someone were actually speaking for her. "Sometimes when I want to speak," she said in the same way, "something comes between my thoughts and the words."'[30] The narrator speaks of her 'private language' in which she imagines but does not speak, and in anger she had accused her mother that 'I might have been a person, but you made me a foreigner', and the narrator comments, 'She would have depended less on words, she would have belonged to life.'[31] These passages are also related to Flor's irrational fears, but she associates the condition of being 'foreign' not only to the exile in Europe, although this has accentuated it, but to an earlier time in America when Bonnie sent her to a school in which she was 'the only Catholic girl'. When Flor overhears American tourists at the Café de la Paix, she thinks, 'they spoke the language she knew best, with the words she had been taught to use when, long ago, she had seen shapes and felt desires that had to be given names.'[32] A phrase from Shakespeare enters her consciousness, but 'she did not say this. Her lips did not move, but she had the ringing impression of a faultless echo. As if the words had come to her in her own voice. They were words out of the old days, when she could still read, and relate every sentence to the sentence it followed.'[33] In fact, the awareness of a loss of her own voice that she mentioned to Bob earlier in their relationship intensifies until these later stages when she experiences a complete alienation from language and expression, and it appears that the inability to read or to think coherently are a prelude to her breakdown.

Gallant's cast of characters in *Green Water, Green Sky* resembles many of her displaced characters in other stories of the 1950s, expatriates in European countries, and her emphasis is again on the condition of exile, but there is another dimension to what afflicts Flor. While Gallant valued her freedom to travel, her personal independence as a woman, and her radical political perspective, her writing, especially its earliest stages, is centrally concerned with those for whom survival and independence are scarcely attainable. Her first published stories in Montreal concern refugees, inspired by Austrian and Czech refugees she had met in the city, and she will often write of displaced persons throughout her career, so much so that an interviewer asked her, 'Do you think everyone is a refugee?' 'It would be too easy to say yes', she replied, 'yet if you move from one social class to another you're a refugee, aren't you? Isn't a religious convert a refugee? Or someone who loses faith in

ideas and people? If you move from one province to another you are a
refugee of a kind. There is always something left behind.'[34] In short, the
answer is yes, but refugee is a term that appears to include all displaced
persons, uprooted, marginalized, exiled, or people simply travelling or
emigrating. Gallant insists that she does not choose such isolated characters; they simply arrive in her imagination, as Flor McCarthy did, but
it is evident that her cast of characters is in various aspects a mirroring
of what she knows in her own experience.

More than this, however, is her concern with the more existential
condition of meaninglessness that arises in absurd circumstances, and
the public circumstance that focused her thinking in her first decades
was the war. 'I am the war generation', Gallant remarked, 'and I was
never satisfied with anything that I had read about it. Everything
seemed to be written in black and white, and I wondered if I could do
something with fiction.'[35] She was responding to a question about
'The Pegnitz Junction', her extraordinary novella of the post-war generation in Germany, written in the late 1960s. But that sense of enquiry
and mission animates not only her 'German' stories for it is not so
much the populations she observes, the displaced North Americans,
the Parisians, the young travellers, or their cultures, which matter; it is
how she goes about using fiction itself as a means of understanding
what might otherwise remain opaque. 'Journalism,' she said, 'recounts
as exactly and economically as possible the weather in the street; fiction takes no notice of that particular weather but brings to life a
distillation of all weathers, a climate of the mind.'[36] Gallant is focused
on something similar to the later enquiry of W. G. Sebald: how does
an imaginative and morally aware individual survive and articulate
the knowledge of what happened in Europe in the mid-twentieth
century? Like Sebald, her 'climate of the mind' is permeated with
knowledge both autobiographical and historical: the individual life
reflects and refracts the cultural, but in the end survival depends on an
independent probing intelligence that refuses any clichés, summaries,
or conclusions.

From the age of eighteen, when she returned to Montreal, Mavis
Gallant was aware of the war as a defining condition of her life in the
city. She felt the war as 'something very claustrophobic', for many men
were serving in the Canadian army in Europe, their wives awaiting
their death or their return. Women were now employed in many jobs
previously reserved for men, and Gallant found opportunities in the

city, especially as a feature writer, but rather than find purpose in the heroic climate of the nation at war, she identified with refugees, abandoned wives, and, later, disoriented war brides. In her play, *What is to be done?*, a young woman declares 'I'm looking for a life' and another replies, 'There's no life anywhere. There's a war.'[37] A highlight of Gallant's career was interviewing Jean-Paul Sartre, but the event of greatest impact appears to have been the arrival through news agencies of photographs of the death camps in 1945. She was asked to provide captions for them, but she refused: she believed the impact of the visual images should not be deflected or mediated by any propagandistic comment. She wanted newspaper readers to come to terms in private, as it were, with the bewildering truth these images represented. 'All I knew, or felt, looking at those pictures was that we had to find out, from the Germans themselves, what had gone wrong. . . . The *why* was desperately important to people like myself who were twenty-two and had to live with this shambles. . . . I never lost interest in what had happened, the why of it, I mean.'[38] More than her personal memories or the fictional war time images of Elizabeth Bowen, these were hallucinations of the real world, of the 'human collapse' that *Green Water, Green Sky* investigates.

Gallant remained in Montreal for another five years, but there is little doubt that her ambition from 1945 was to go to Europe, to find out for herself what lay behind the 'black and white' accounts of the war. 'We couldn't take it in', Gallant said. 'Once I got on the subject, I wanted to go to the very end of it.'[39] Asked if she can identify the features of her own style, she insists she never rereads her stories and cannot answer, but when she did in the case of two stories, she found them to be characterized by 'loss and bewilderment'. The authority structures of family, religious or political beliefs, or local cultural histories, no longer offer security or moral guidance to adults 'in transit'. The systematic savagery of the Second World War undermined all traditional assumptions, and it is not only her German characters, such as the young woman Christine in 'The Pegnitz Junction', who are incapable of identifying what they feel or think in the aftermath of the death camps. Soon after writing *Green Water, Green Sky*, Gallant began a project of research by travelling frequently in Germany for many years, and out of this project of the early 1960s came her German stories.

Gallant does not overtly make Flor aware of the devastation of the post-war landscape, or of the displaced persons in camps around

Europe, although it is remarkable that the first scene in Venice takes place in 1946 or 1947, so that the detail that Bob's father came from the Warsaw ghetto surely echoes Gallant's visceral response to the images from liberated Poland. In this fiction, what is excluded from the depiction of Europe at this historical moment is both a comment on the insulated world of the American expatriates and perhaps a silent acknowledgement of the unspeakable. During an attack of vertigo in front of the Café de la Paix, Flor concludes that her existential condition of despair and meaninglessness was always a part of her, that it is not only due to the historical circumstances of post-war Europe or expatriate Americans, in fact, but a deeper aspect of the human condition. The epigraph from Shakespeare, from a romance comedy of exile, confused identity and disguise, and the words of the fool, 'travellers must be content', seem to provide a motto for these homeless travellers, but in the play the circumstances that lead to exile are governed by violence and arrogant power. There is a more telling quotation from Shakespeare which Flor, in extremis, recalls at the Café de la Paix, from *Timon of Athens*, which focuses on even more violent and despairing circumstances. This is Shakespeare writing in a tragic mode, and the words of Timon in despair suggest that suicide may be the only possible response. This quotation, taken from the context of war, is even closer to Flor's state of mind than the lines from *As You Like It*.

If Gallant's material lends itself to tragedy and elegy, the unspeakable historical circumstances and the personal collapse, the writer finds in herself the determination to create a language and a voice that are a sign of the moral strength to counter fascisms in everyday life and to create a literary art that is singularly authentic.

~

Green Water, Green Sky situates these related issues of language, voice, exile, and coercion in a larger exploration of literature and the writing of fiction, and it is in this sense that it is energized by central autobiographical questions. Flor's loss of language, associated with other kinds of loss, mirrors many key elements of Gallant's own childhood and youth, and so this fiction explores those elements of loss and the foundation for the recovery of personal independence and an authentic voice in writing.

During the opening scene in Venice, Bonnie tells George that her husband, Stanley, 'had been so dreadful to her, he had humiliated her so deeply that she couldn't live in America. . . . She was condemned to live abroad and bring Flor up in some harmful way: harmful for Flor, that is.'[40] It is evident already that Bonnie is an unreliable witness. Flor's tension as her mother speaks is linked to George's stammer, a physical manifestation of a loss of voice, and both children are conscious of having to work out the truth of events for themselves since adults construct self-justifying façades and narratives. Flor tells George later that "'She'd had this man around for ages, this doctor, so she couldn't complain.... Stanley never said anything and then all of a sudden he blew up and threw her out.'"[41] George has met his Uncle Stanley and his new wife, and Flor is hungry for information about her father. 'In George's memory it was here that Florence cried: "She'll never do anything any more. I'll always keep her with me.".... She meant these words, they weren't intended for George. It was a solemn promise, a cry of despair, love and resentment so closely woven together that even Flor couldn't tell them apart.'[42] At age seven, George is already troublingly aware of the price Flor is paying for this arrangement as he notes her erratic gestures, her anger, and her destructive impulses.

Over the decade that follows, as revealed in Part II, Flor's psychic imprisonment in her mother's egocentric life intensifies. Physical symptoms of estrangement, such as attacks of vertigo and her inability to conceive a child are metaphors for her psychological state. She becomes so estranged from her mother and her husband that she withdraws into a silent world with her own 'private language' of dream images, in particular one of being controlled by a fox. Part II ends with a fantasy of escaping from the fox and riding a pony through the woods: 'She held herself straight. She was perfect. Everyone smiled now. Everyone was pleased. She emerged in triumph from the little wood and came off Chief, her pony, and into her father's arms.'[43] Only in Part IV does the reader discover that Flor's wish will not be realized for soon after she had been admitted to an asylum.

There are a number of echoes here of the disintegration of Gallant's own family. In 'The Doctor', one of the Linnet Muir series—a set of six memoir-stories which, Gallant explained, were 'as close to autobiography as fiction can be'[44]—Linnet senses that her flamboyant mother, and perhaps her father too, have special relationships with close friends.

Unconsciously, everyone under the age of ten knows everything. Under-ten can come into a room and sense at once everything felt, kept silent, held back in the way of love, hate, and desire though he may not have the right words for such sentiments. It is part of the clairvoyant immunity to hypocrisy we are born with and that vanishes just before puberty. I knew, though no one had told me, that my mother was a bit foolish about Dr. Chauchard.[45]

This intuitive knowledge is dramatized in many stories of children, who are almost always female, and it shapes the conception of those sensitive and searching characters, the young women who are protagonists of the longer fictions.

The 'clairvoyant' ability to know the unstated truth is surely linked in Gallant to the imaginative and poetic insights that are associated with the practice of art. Yet if children are capable of such intuitive knowledge, it is often frustratingly incomplete, and the adult self may be motivated to pierce those mysteries that have endured since childhood. In the case of 'The Doctor', the adult Linnet must revise her understanding of his identity.

'Think of your unfortunate parents,' Dr. Chauchard had said in the sort of language that had no meaning to me, though I'm sure it was authentic to him. When he died and I read his obituary, I saw there had been still another voice.... That third notice [obituary] was an earthquake, the collapse of the cities we build over the past to cover seams and cracks we cannot account for.[46]

Linnet discovers that he had been a celebrated French-language poet: 'I am sure that it was his real voice, the voice that transcends this or that language.... I ought to have heard it when I was still under ten and had all my wits about me.'[47] Linnet's regret that she had not known that 'real voice', that she had been too preoccupied with his social and professional roles, is modified to a degree by the fact that the doctor's English-speaking friends had not known of his work as poet either, but this simply reinforces the idea that art, like childhood fantasies and intuitions, exists in a world apart from ordinary social uses of language.

The father's disappearance is the central mystery in the lives of Linnet and of Gallant and marks the boundary between childhood and the stage of 'loss and bewilderment' that follows. Gallant refers to her father as 'the empty chair', the abiding sense of absence, and when, at the age of eighteen, she returns to Montreal to have an independent life, her first goal is to solve the mystery of her father's disappearance, 'to confront the free adult world of falsehood and evasion on an equal footing'.[48] In the first Linnet Muir story, 'In Youth is Pleasure', Linnet recalls making appointments to meet former friends of her father, such as

Angus: 'First it was light chatter, then darker gossip, and then it went too far (*he* was ill and he couldn't hide it; *she* had a lover and didn't try); then suddenly it became tragic, and open tragedy was disallowed.'[49] The various scenarios she hears are not consistent or complete:

I arrived at something about tuberculosis of the spine and a butchery of an operation. He started back to England to die there but either changed his mind or was too ill to begin the journey: at Quebec City where he was to have taken ship, he shot himself in a public park at five o'clock in the morning. That was one version; another was that he had died at sea and the gun was found in his luggage.[50]

These various scenarios are situated in the context of the parents' foundering marriage (the taciturn father in contrast to the mother, who 'made herself the central figure in loud, spectacular dramas which she played with the houselights on'), but Linnet Muir, first-person narrator, does not blame anyone: 'I had settled his fate in my mind and I never varied: I thought he had died of homesickness; sickness for England was the consumption, the gun, the everything.... Once I had made up my mind, the whole story somehow became none of my business.'[51]

In other words, she imagines her father as fundamentally a displaced person in Montreal, suffering a variety of exile, like one of the characters in another Linnet Muir story of that title. There is a suggestion there that his exile may have been dishonourable in some way, that he was a kind of 'remittance man' banished out of shame by his repressed and taciturn Anglo-Scottish family. Yet at the end of that story, she questions her compulsion to write stories: 'All this business of putting life through a sieve and then discarding it was another variety of exile; I knew that even then, but it seemed quite right and perfectly natural.'[52] This moment of ambivalent self-knowledge for Linnet Muir and Gallant the writer in exile echoes another moment of similar import in *Green Water, Green Sky* quoted earlier: '[Flor] would have depended less on words. She would have belonged to life.' The compulsion to understand, to translate mystery into words, is what compels the homeless one to write, and yet the gap between 'words' and 'life', although it is 'perfectly natural', appears to compound the sense of alienation.

Linnet Muir's need to solve the mystery of her father continues, even though at the age of eighteen, in the first story, she had concluded it was none of her business. In fact, it is suggested in another Linnet

Muir story that it was fundamental to her writing, and especially to the issue of an 'authentic voice'. 'Voices Lost in Snow' begins with an abrupt warning: 'Dark riddles filled the corners of life because no enlightenment was thought required.'[53] Parents do not welcome questions from children, and answers are abrupt and final: 'Observe the drift of words descending from adult to child. . . . He must hear the voice of authority muffled, a hum through snow.'[54] While Linnet generalizes about all adult voices, her own conversation with her father is included, 'their voices lost in snow' and yet, clearly alluding to her father, she remarks, 'the only authentic voices I have belong to the dead'.[55]

The story recounts an afternoon visit to Linnet's godmother, Georgie, now estranged from Linnet's mother, as they both know they are rivals for her father's attentions. It is set just a year before her father's disappearance from her life, and while its tone is marked by anger directed at the silencing, evasive style of parents' communications, there is also an embedded elegy here for the father: 'I don't look back at anything being very hard except the death of my father and my mother's remarriage and her abandonment of me. I found it very hard to be in the world without a father.'[56] His few words, even when they advocate silence, were the last words she can recall and so they assume an aura of authenticity. Later, acknowledging the child's discomfort, he remarks, '"You didn't enjoy your visit very much. . . . You needn't see Georgie again unless you want to."'[57] The words seem to offer a revelation of another dimension in her father's character, but when she asks why, the conventional answer returns: '"Because I say so."' They are her father's final words, in her recollection: 'The answer seems to speak out of the lights, the stones, the snow; out of the crucial second when inner and outer forces join, and the environment becomes part of the enemy too.' Just before, as they walk down the snowy street together, the adult narrator comments that her ailing father at this time may have been 'stifling pain in silence rather than speaking up while there might have been time': 'he gave an impression of sternness that was a shield against suffering.' This afternoon may have been a crucial and final one for him too; Linnet now realizes that he may have taken 'a private decision about himself'. What he concealed from her with 'Because I say so' was the hidden crisis in his own life which he cannot share with her in words. It is implied that he shared it with her anyway, unarticulated but intuitively felt by the child. Linnet, at first so determined to penetrate to the truth of her childhood, seems to realize that all she has are speculations,

uncertainties, fragmentary memories that may be arranged into a narrative, but that chance and mystery occupy a dark background. The
story is designed as an exemplification of the truth that the child is
inevitably trapped in 'snow', opaque language, and that the surfaces of
daily communication are enigmatic and estranging. Yet it also defines
the role of the adult narrator/writer: to situate the reader in a parallel
relationship to language so that the drama of reading is experienced as
an interplay between what is revealed and what is concealed, between
what is knowable and what remains mysterious.[58]

In Gallant's Preface to the *Selected Stories*, she dates the origins of her
impulse and need to be a writer to her earliest years as an only child:
'I have been writing or just thinking about things to write since I was
a child. I invented rhymes and stories when I could not get to sleep
and in the morning when I was told it was too early to get up.'[59] She
still believes that 'it is child's play, an extension of make-believe', but it
is not the accident of the child's circumstances that interests her; it is
that a child has a special quality of mind: 'perhaps a writer is a child in
disguise, with a child's lucid view of grown-ups, accurate as to atmosphere, improvising when it tries to make sense of adult behaviour.'[60]
The child has an intuition of what is not articulated in her hearing, or
perhaps not articulated at all because adults' feelings and desires are
often concealed, repressed, feared, or avoided; and Gallant appears to
believe that the truth of the child's intuition is to be trusted more than
adult rationalizations, explanations, and obfuscations.

Gallant's impassioned detachment and relentless search for truth
'with a capital T', as one of the Linnet Muir stories is entitled, owes
something to her early years as a journalist. As 'Voices Lost in Snow'
suggests, the wintry climate of the Montreal streets is actually a metaphor for the inner condition that settled in Linnet's sense of her father's
absence, 'the climate of the mind'. Yet the outer and the inner conditions are the fabric of the fiction, and the voice of the writer is present
in the narrative voice of the older Linnet. She is an investigator, a
researcher, an impassioned interrogator of details, a sifter of nuances
and perspectives, but the need for the *mot juste* is all the greater because
it will never quite penetrate the 'dark riddles'.

～

'Childhood recollected is often hallucination.' These are the opening
words of 'Rose', published in 1960, although this is one of a number
of stories first written in the 1940s, packed away and rediscovered

by Gallant in the late 1950s. The young narrator, Irmgard, recalls an incident from childhood in Quebec, and she reappears in another story of a childhood incident, 'Jorinda and Jorindel', both stories, presumably reworked, published within a year of the stories of Flor. Both are set in a country house near the Canadian–American border, and in each, the family situation is similar and there are older cousins from Boston, in one case a boy, in the other a girl. Their presence is used to indicate contrasts of background or inheritance in Irmgard's family and even more to reveal the kinds of unease Irmgard is absorbing in her confusing world. A third story of a young girl in a country house, 'The Wedding Ring', is closely related to these two and all of them provide further insight into Gallant's early development, written closer to the actual experiences than the memoir stories of Linnet Muir of the mid-1970s. The material of a fracturing marriage and an anxious child observing everything, imagining explanations, wishing for understanding, is close to that of 'Voices Lost in Snow' and 'The Doctor' later; in certain ways, however, these early stories focused on the mother open up further contexts for the origins of *Green Water, Green Sky*.

The 'hallucination' that is the subject of 'Rose' appears to be linked to doubleness and dual cultural norms and to a child with an over-stimulated imagination. 'I had never been told the Boston cousin [Rose] existed', Irmgard remarks, 'but I knew. I knew about it although no one had told me a thing. Perhaps that intuitive knowledge, the piecing together of facts overheard, overcharges the mind.'[61] Irmgard is taken by her nursemaid to visit her maternal grandmother in Vermont: 'we cross the border, where there is a different way of speaking, different money, a different flag.' This journey seems to dramatize the inherent contradictions in the child's immediate experience—and many details are taken from Gallant's own life: Irmgard goes to a Catholic *pensionnat*, although her parents 'are atheists' and her grandmother is 'socialist, bluestocking, agnostic and a snob'. The occasion of the journey is Christmas, the traditional celebrations of which her parents have rejected, although at the convent school the child is exposed to 'four weeks of fever' leading up to the religious festival. She appears to be named in honour of her German grandmother, and at the house in Vermont Irmgard unexpectedly enters a traditional Christmas celebration with all the trappings of a northern European ritual.

In this setting, precisely evoked in details and yet with elements of a fairy tale, 'the hallucination begins'. Rose, a girl of about thirteen, is there, alone, with the grandmother, and their relationship appears to be magically intimate, although Rose is crying; and then she disappears. 'It has the true quality of a hallucination, because I take no part. I can see them, but they cannot see me.'[62] Irmgard knows she has become aware of dimensions in her grandmother's life which she cannot understand, other than as manifestations of the puzzling grown-up world. She knows that she has a wicked, lawless uncle, who lives in Mexico, and has concluded that a daughter of one of his bigamous marriages lives in Boston. But the grandmother's indulgence of her scandalous son leads now to this intimacy with Rose which Irmgard feels is totally out of character for her stern grandmother. The vision provokes not only jealousy but confusion about the disorder of the adult world and a sense of deep division:

Was this grandmother mine, or Rose's? Was her Germany the dark spruce-scented cave, of which I was given a glimpse, or the shadeless landscape, the clear lemon sun? Did Rose carry hers all her life as I did mine—hers mournful, mine sad; hers tearful, mine grim; her (sic) rich, mine thin? But here is the problem, and why it can never be answered: I never saw Rose at all.[63]

The adult narrator elaborates briefly on this twilight zone of reality and imagination, of hallucinations, but the element of mystery enveloping her grandmother remains, and central to that mystery for the child was language: 'there was a heavy brown veil between us—the German tongue. I knew two words for everything, one in English and one in French. I could not admit three.'[64] When her grandmother reads to her in German, with the intention of instructing her, Irmgard associates this cold, Northern woman with the 'lemon sun', so that in her vision of Rose, she imagines a warm, intimate, 'maternal' and protective side to her. It is striking that Irmgard's parents are absent, and she is in the care of Germaine, whom in retrospect she does not trust as a witness of the scene for she was 'simple-minded, and notorious for making legends last'.[65]

The second story of Irmgard, 'Jorinda and Jorindel', is equally concerned with the dissolving condition of realism overlaid with dream and fantasy, as the title's reference to Grimm's fairy tale of a witch who transforms children into birds makes clear. The family situation is similar: Germaine is her nursemaid—'She will never be given anything even approaching Germaine's unmeasured love again'; there is a cousin, Bradley, from Boston; it is holiday time, August at a country house; but now the confusion and division Irmgard experiences is focused on the contrast between her English-speaking, American cousin and an orphaned *Québécois* boy on a neighbouring farm whom she has befriended and who disappears. She feels she has betrayed him, unable to bring the two boys together and forced to choose one. Irmgard's friendship with the boy is largely silent, and appears to be intensified by water, for Irmgard teaches him to swim: 'He does not know the names of flowers, and does not distinguish between the colors green and blue. The apparitions of the Virgin, which are commonplace, take place against a heaven he says is "*vert*." Now, Bradley has never had a vision, and if he did he wouldn't know what it was. He has no trouble explaining anything.'[66] She chooses to spend her time with Bradley, although it is clear that her warmest feelings are for Alfred, and that her American cousin's pragmatic outlook is set against the impoverished and abused boy who stimulates her imagination with his belief in visions. Irmgard has disturbing dreams, including a nightmare about being kidnapped, and the background to these portraits of lost children is of partying grown-ups. There is a striking image of the mother: 'the mother is the mirror, and everything is reflected or darkened, given life or dismissed, in the picture the mother returns. The lake, the house, the summer, the reason for doing one thing instead of another are reflected here, explained, clarified. If the mirror breaks, everything will break, too.'[67] The image of the mirror is used frequently by Gallant at this time, not only in 'Its Image on the Mirror' but in *Green Water, Green Sky*, in which it might be said that Bonnie has much of the power attributed here to the mother to make or shatter these in-between worlds in which feelings of isolation and confusion are registered. The child, perhaps yearning for visionary or absolute knowledge, exists in a natural state of shadows and reflections between water and sky.

A third story, 'The Wedding Ring', also investigates this girl's summertime world at the country house, and it includes other striking images which reappear in the stories of Flor, including this one of the power of the mother to make the child's world cohere or to shatter it. 'That is absolutely my mother', Gallant remarked.[68] Again, the adults are partying, the boy cousin from Boston is present, and the narrator observes:

He is ready for anything except my mother, who scares him to death. My mother is a vixen. Everyone who sees her that summer will remember, later, the gold of her eyes and the lovely movement of her head. Her hair is true russet. . . . She can be wild, bitter, complaining, and ugly as a witch, but that summer is her peak. She has fallen in love.[69]

The girl's father is absent in Montreal and the mother's boyfriend is staying. She observes her mother trying to impress him with her life-story, 'her favourite theme—her lack of roots'. She listens and is aware of her mother's elisions of the truth for the sake of the drama:

'My father and mother didn't get along, and that prevented me feeling close to any country,' says my mother. . . . 'I was divorced from the landscape as they were from each other. I was too taken up with wondering what was going to happen next. . . . My father was dead and my mother was less tense and I was free of their troubles. That is the truth,' she says, with some astonishment.[70]

The mirroring effect, the mother's unreliable version of her life closer perhaps to the story of her own daughter's life, her characterization as a witch and as a fox draw these fictions close to the stories of Flor, the final image perhaps most of all.

The girl leaves for Boston with her cousin, and yet it is as if she remained at the country house to experience the shattering of her world for ever, the definitive hallucination:

Uncut grass. I saw the ring fall into it, but I am told I did not—I was already in Boston. The weekend party, her chosen audience, watched her rise, without warning, from the wicker chair on the porch. An admirer of Russian novels, she would love to make an immediate, Russian, gesture, but cannot. The porch is screened, so, to throw her wedding ring away, she must have walked a few steps to the door and *then* made her speech, and flung the ring into the twilight, in a great spinning arc.[71]

The characterization of Bonnie is suggested but also of Flor destroying the necklace in Venice; indeed, it is as if the mother-vixen becomes the fox that haunts and takes possession of Flor. The final line of the story resonates: 'My mother's hands were small, like mine.'[72] The ring was never found in the grass, but the narrator's yearning for some kind of identification with the mother that she can grasp is clear. The finality of the dramatic gesture, the overwhelming need for personal independence at any price, the smashing of something for ever all seem to echo Flor's life and the complex blurring of identities between her and Bonnie, and yet only through total withdrawal can she even begin to become independent of her mother. In these stories, as daughters absorb their mother's personality and ambience, it is only the narrator who achieves independence and represents it by creating a narrative style that establishes a poised distance from the unreal world of shadows, reflections and mirrorings, represented by the title image, Green Water, Green Sky.

'Gallant thinks her emotionally truncated childhood has found its way into her fiction,' Sandra Martin remarked in a profile and then quotes Gallant on her mother's abandonment of her following her father's disappearance: 'She wanted a completely new life. And I was not only part of this other life, but I was the image of my father, in temperament, in appearance, in manner, in voice—a kind of living reproach.'[73] The Linnet Muir memoir-stories explicitly foreground the young woman who set about discovering the truth of her father's life, whereas it seems that in these stories of childhood, Gallant is searching to understand the mother–daughter relationship. It ended abrasively, and Gallant is sympathetic in this statement and elsewhere towards her mother, but it is also clear that what she absorbed in the confusion of her childhood, in its intuitive and hallucinatory modes of understanding, provided her with a powerful sense of identification with her father. He was the artist figure, and the mother is introduced as a reader, especially of classical Russian fiction. If Mavis Gallant resembled her father physically, even to having his voice, there is no doubt that her mother too was intellectually inclined, drawn to the arts and to a community of like-minded, somewhat bohemian, people in Montreal. Memories of the father are exclusively anchored in childhood, before the age of ten, whereas her mother remained to a degree active in her life into her adolescence, and so the images from childhood were overlaid by later experiences of an unhappy and conflicted relationship. The silent and invisible father became one kind of reality that Gallant's imagination could play on, whereas the mother's active and interfering presence was a different kind of reality, and with these Quebec stories as prompts, it is not difficult to imagine that Bonnie Fairlee from New York may be partially modelled on Gallant's mother.

Biographical information about Gallant's mother is scarce; that there is contradictory evidence about her nationality, American or Canadian, is appropriate in the light of the Irmgard stories with border crossings and American cousins. Gallant always insisted on her Canadian citizenship and that she had never considered getting any other passport, implying that she might have done so, but her childhood and adolescence appears to have been clouded, and while the unusual overlapping of

English and French languages in her formation is clear, there is also an overlapping of Canada and the United States in her formation. Gallant's first story considered by the *New Yorker* was rejected because it was too limited by its Canadian material, and so Gallant began to write 'American' stories. It does not appear to have caused her any difficulty to write of American characters at home or in Europe, and she continued to do this through the 1950s until close to the publication of *Green Water, Green Sky*, when the first stories set in Montreal appeared.

~

In Part IV, George's discovery of his own imaginative and intellectual resources for making sense of what he finds are exemplified on this short evening in Paris. He is clear-sighted in his observations of Bonnie and Bob. He is even frank and direct in voicing his feelings and thoughts. Recognizing his aunt's hypocrisy and contradictory self-serving declarations, he checks her: "'*You* didn't have to live with her," George said. It was the kind of statement that went out of his mouth before it was through his mind.'[74] It is clear to him that a major problem for the young couple has been Bonnie's presence and constant interference.

George put himself in Harris's place and felt sick.... They seemed bewildered. Each was the witness of the other's suffering and that must have been terrible to bear. Harris probably wasn't taking in half the foolish things she said. He looked like a man who had come into a known station only to find all the trains going to the wrong places or leaving at impossible times: endlessly patient, he was waiting for the schedules to be rearranged.[75]

What hope does Harris have of finding a way? George is sympathetic to his dilemma. 'His voice was soft, for a man, full of the sounds and rhythms that meant New York. This came over to George with wild familiarity. Across Paris, the voice conveyed the existence of seasons, mornings, afternoons...Everything pertaining to danger and grief flowed and settled around that talk.'[76] While George recognizes the unreal world in which Harris finds himself—imagery of maps and trains surely anticipates the basic idea of the journey through a nightmare landscape in 'The Pegnitz Junction'—he also sees Harris's limitations. 'They seemed to be joined for life, and, before thinking and deciding not to say it, George said, "God, I feel sorry for you, Bob"...Presently he realized that what Bob had said bore no relation to George's remark. It was simply a statement given into the night.'[77] A short time earlier, a young woman has passed them on the street: "'Nursemaid," said

Bonnie into the night. "Millions of them come from Scandinavia every year. Warm little loves. They are supposed to be learning French."[78] George's honest and spontaneous reactions are deflated by these remarks 'into the night' so that he realized neither Bonnie nor Bob can actually hear what he wants to say or have a serious conversation. He is on his own, and this is why he must leave them.

While George himself is at sea on his first trip alone to London—where he frankly confesses to having been lonely—and to Paris, he is capable of recognizing the desolation of Bonnie and Bob, and has an intuitive sense of its causes and its consequences. In their company on this evening, he is capable of detaching himself and seeing them from a distance. He responds to textures of voices and to visual images, and he appears to have learned to do this as a child from his first observations of Flor:

George remembered what it had been like to be with Flor just as, through a hole in time, one goes back to a lake, a room in a city, or the south. It was probably because of the bead.... When he thought about his cousin that was what he saw: a thin sunburned girl pulling on a string of beads and making the string break...she was fixed then and now and for all his life: a wild girl breaking a necklace, the circle of life closing in at fourteen, the family, the mother, the husband to come.[79]

This incident on the day of his abandonment in Venice was 'a prophetic moment', a foundational moment in his imaginative engagement with Flor's life. More than that, he discovered a moral sense and an understanding of the fundamental condition of alienation.

On this evening, he considers Flor's situation:

Flor was not anywhere now, so perhaps it didn't matter. Perhaps it was courtesy to accept the mother's mistakes. But he was stubborn and he knew that his isolated memories of Flor were right and Aunt Bonnie's fantasies wrong.... Bob, encased in silence and false calm, knew even more; but it was better not to explore that country.[80]

His recollection of Flor's expression of her embedded anger in destroying the necklace, in revolting against her imprisonment with Bonnie, allows him to grasp her isolation and homelessness. In a sense, she is an image of the loss of identity in such circumstances.

Wondering where she was *really* he suspected she was in no special place. She was not anywhere. It would be nice to believe she was happier, calmer, more loving than ever, but he thought she was not anywhere. The minute George went too far in his speculations he lost hold of the real situation. He could see three people walking, stopping for traffic, moving on. He could hear their voices, but he could not understand any of the things they said.[81]

Remarkably, as he reaches a limit of his thinking, George is described as experiencing her condition, 'not anywhere', the disassociation of voice from meaning. This image of the disintegration of the possibility of communicating or understanding as they walk the streets of Paris, anticipates the recognition of limits of Linnet Muir as she walks with her father and is aware of 'voices lost in snow'. The buildings of Paris, the many named streets they walk on, the lights and the night, all dissolve into a new kind of perception for George.

Earlier, 'his eyes met the eyes of a girl coming towards them. The girl emerged in the most poetic way imaginable, out of the Paris night. That was the way he wanted something to happen; that was the thing he was ready for now.'[82] Bonnie dismisses the girl as a prostitute, and, indeed, Paris itself is also referred to as a prostitute. But, in the final paragraph of the fiction, after George has realized that he is powerless to do anything for Flor and has decided to leave Bonnie and Bob, he has an 'authentic hallucination': 'He saw Aunt Bonnie and Flor and the girl on the Quai Anatole France as one person. She was a changeable figure, now menacing, now dear; a minute later behaving like a queen in exile, plaintive and haughty, eccentric by birth, unaware, or not caring, that the others were laughing behind their hands.'[83] His 'hallucination', his fusion of characters in a kaleidoscopic figure, comes remarkably close to the painterly effect of Gallant's own style in this fiction, *Green Water, Green Sky*.[84]

~

Green Water, Green Sky is the first in a series of difficult experimental narratives, each of which focuses on a young woman. I believe they form the backbone of Gallant's accomplishment and allow us to understand something of the wellsprings of her art in her own odyssey. They may be seen as a means of reconciling her inner and outer worlds, her own private misery and the desolation she came to know in observing social relationships and in the large-scale savagery of wartime Europe. They represent 'the climate of [her] mind'. More than this, these fictions may be seen as successive explorations in the evolution of a style and the beliefs that underlie it, contributions to an understanding of why personal independence matters. I believe it is very much in character for Gallant not to write 'A Portrait of the Artist as a Young Woman', but rather to write sets of related fictions with multiple, discontinuous perspectives in time and in the angle of vision, a kind of cubism in prose. In this respect, Gallant's remark to Michel Fabre is pertinent, 'The events and characters in fiction are like works of art in a museum. You see them from different angles, you move round and around. You don't stand at the same place.'[85]

In 'Its Image on the Mirror', written at about the same time as *Green Water, Green Sky*, the characterization of Jean Price, bewildered by life in wartime Montreal and lacking personal independence, might be designed to portray another person Gallant is determined not to become. The novella is remarkable for its recreation of a family absorbing the impact of war, and the complexity of its treatment of time, memory, and identity reveals how much the issues at stake matter and the art that needs to be created for their investigation. Essentially, Jean Price realizes that her family of origin and her cultural milieu in English Quebec are both disintegrating, her social and moral anchors in the world have become obsolete, and she lives in a state of isolation and loss. 'It seemed to me I had waited years for life to begin and that the false start of the after-war was all there had been to wait for',[86] and her defensive relationships with her husband and her sister, Isobel, dramatize her failure to discover love or vitality; in fact, she is helplessly jealous of Isobel's ability to have an independent and passionate life. Her beloved brother is killed in the war, and the war is the greater condition of death that makes personal vulnerability and authenticity the ground on which a new existential life will need to be created. But Jean Price is not the person to achieve this. 'There is no condition of snow I have not observed, from the first fall to the mild deceptive stillness at night, close to the end of winter, when a dark breath, indrawn and held, warns that death is returning after all.'[87] After her brother's death, she feels that she is 'obliged to survive', but 'we slipped into our winter as trustingly as every night we fell asleep', and, although it is evident that Isobel has survived by starting a new life far away from her upbringing, Jean will not really 'survive'.

Nor will Flor, or Shirley, the young woman in the novel *A Fairly Good Time* (1970), or Christine in 'The Pegnitz Junction', the novella set in Germany and which is accompanied by a set of 'German' stories in the volume of that name (1973). All these young women are presented in states close to breakdown, overwhelmed by the dissolving reality of historical contexts, the voices lost in snow—an image not only of Linnet Muir and her father on a winter street in Montreal but,

from the late 1950s on, an image of the vulnerability of the single life
to the enveloping forces of death and disappearance. Most salient in
all these fictions is her deepest concern in those years: the failure of
European intellectual and cultural traditions to recognize and limit
the rise of Nazi barbarism. Gallant's personal sense of exile and abandonment prepared her for this wider concern with European cultural
conditions that might be articulated only to a small degree in the
individual characters of her fiction but which actually permeated the
landscape. Her fiction is markedly different from that of Henry James,
in that her Venice, her Cannes and Paris have lost all romantic glamour,
although North Americans still visit these cities. The vulnerability of
individual exiles is intensified by the reduction of such places to an
unreal and shadowed world pressing in on them, much like the London
at night-time that Elizabeth Bowen's characters experience in
'Mysterious Kor' or Gallant's experience of Franco's Spain.[88]

Green Water, Green Sky is incoherent in conventional narrative terms
and incomplete, but the omniscient narrative voice holds this incoherence in suspense. The 'climate of [Flor's] mind' is revealed directly in
passages focus on her or on the perceptions of others and, indirectly, often contrastingly, in the varieties of exile and purposefulness
of others, and in particular in the complementary portraits of Flor and
George. The portrait of the young woman is unfinished and many
riddles remain, and in this way the oblique style of writing anticipates
the later portraits. It is only in the extended set of Linnet Muir fictions
that Gallant is finally explicit about her investigative method, her
motivation, and her recognition of narrative limits. 'Gallant retains
such a tenacious grip on perspective that the narrative voice unobtru-
sively but unwaveringly guides the reader in and around and through
these events and characters as they are perceived from different angles.'[89]
This critic's aim is to situate Gallant's writing and the reader's perception of the work in terms of the visual arts, and this is certainly useful,
but there is a tension in the narrative voice between omniscience and
riddle, a recognition that language must call on poetic means to establish the primary reality of mystery, death, and silence. The complex
elaboration of metaphors such as snow, water, and light permeates the
realistic and representational textures of the fiction, yet it is in Gallant's
confident narrative voice and the depth and clarity of conviction
underlying her enterprise in fiction that she takes the reader far beyond
the black and white understanding she rejected at an early age.

5

J. M. Coetzee's *Dusklands*
'The voice of the doubting self'

J. M. Coetzee has spoken of the 'massive autobiographical writing enterprise that fills a life',[1] and in his own case he has characterized that life-long dedication to his art as 'something constitutional to the writer, what one might loosely call conscience but what I would tentatively prefer to call an imperative, a transcendental imperative'.[2] He has also spoken of the way 'one's life and one's vocation begin to merge'[3] so that 'a life in writing' implies that while writing itself becomes central to the autobiographical enterprise, it is not a transcription of a prior understanding or truth, nor does it represent the voice of an achieved self; rather, autobiography is a search for that authentic self and whatever truth may be discovered in the process. In paying homage to Rilke, an early mentor, he explained what he valued in the poet:

> He meant a certain intensity and inwardness, qualities I could swear I heard in the German itself; images, insights . . . being pushed to what one thought was their limit and then beyond that limit into a space of what I can only call magisterial freedom, yet his pushing of the image, audible, almost tangible, being achieved without strain, effortlessly.[4]

This 'transcendental imperative' in Rilke, something Coetzee responded to in many other artists also, is grounded in poetic language, the free self articulating its own style, yet the recalcitrance of the daily world, the authoritarianism of cultural and political regimes, was his earliest experience in South Africa. And so, the 'conscience' of Coetzee first grounded his search for 'magisterial freedom' in a resistance to the imprisoning circumstances of his original Afrikaans culture and its regime of apartheid, and in the voices of that culture. His first work of fiction, *Dusklands*, already sets the foundations of his search for his own authentic voice in the face of the silencing powers of received historical and cultural orthodoxies. Four decades later, it is also evident that this novel initiated a life-long concern with secular confession, self-knowledge, and how literature may discover truth in its own terms.

Published in 1974 in South Africa, *Dusklands* consists of two separate fictions, 'The Vietnam Project' and 'The Narrative of Jacobus Coetzee'.[5] 'The Narrative' was written first. It is presented as a memoir set in 1760, originally written in Dutch, accompanied by a scholarly 'Introduction', apparently published in a previous edition in 1951, in Afrikaans, and accompanied also by a brief 'Translator's Preface'. This 'translator' is identified as 'J. M. Coetzee', although it is clear that, as in Defoe's many fictions, these documents are indeed brilliantly realized forgeries, including the adaptation of a transcript, in an Appendix, of a brief Deposition in 1760 by an illiterate explorer named Jacobus Coetzee.[6] Clearly, all are unreliable interpreters of the reality of historical experience in South Africa, yet Coetzee's interest is not only in the blindness to barbarism which 'The Narrative' reveals: he is interested in how ways of thinking and feeling are represented and misrepresented in written texts. 'The Vietnam Project' extends this concern. The second fiction is a monologue set in 1973 in California, a confessional self-justification, spoken in an urgent and arrogant voice by an unreliable narrator. An expert in psychological warfare, working for the American army, Eugene Dawn's personal and professional lives have imploded, and yet in spite of his effort to maintain a rational poise as narrator, his work and his violent act against his son reveal a profound alienation. Although the experiment in writing a historical fiction engaged Coetzee deeply for a long period of time, in *Dusklands* he placed 'The Vietnam Project' first, as if to indicate that the perennial issues of selfhood and expression were as central to the understanding of imperial America as to the original Dutch colony in South Africa.

The layering of voices in 'The Narrative of Jacobus Coetzee', of historical witnesses, as it were, along with the reader's realization that none of these voices represents the authorial voice, creates an enigmatic play with the conventions of literary and historical narration. Although the characters speak and write in a kind of echo-chamber in literary history, the elusive presence of an author is felt, an impassioned author, for both fictions in *Dusklands* operate at a high stylistic voltage permeated by various kinds of irony. In the interest of preserving the visceral impact of these dramatized single voices, Coetzee worked hard to conceal an omniscient voice that might replace the burden of inter-pretation that falls on the reader. Speaking of the early impact of poets like Eliot, Pound, and other modernists whose style forced the reader to slow down, he insists that prose too has resources to slow down the reader: 'it ought never to be impossible to get the voice into prose, not perhaps the voice that speaks from the throat and chest (that remains the property of verse), but at least what I might call the voice of the mind, the voice in the mind.'[7] His main example is Beckett, in whose best work Coetzee found 'an energy of quite a savage order, under the control of a syntax of the utmost lucidity'.[8] This discovery was part of what happened in his early twenties, at that stage when 'one begins, almost inevitably, to define or at least to demarcate an identity for oneself', and this is a time, he continues, when 'one is more acutely sensitive and receptive to rhythms, tones, melodies, including the rhythms and tones of language, than at any time before or after'.[9] Coetzee's autobiographical reflections on his formation as a writer, his 'homage' to the great writers, 'without whom I would, in a certain sense, not exist', refers only to their use of language and insists that 'my predominating sensory orientation in those days remained aural'.[10]

   From the beginning of Coetzee's career, it is evident that his impas-sioned and engaged fictions are written as complex dramatizations of voices, and the relationship between narrative voices and Coetzee's own 'writing voice'—'the voice in the mind'—gradually emerges in its many variations over the following decades. It is in this light that the far-reaching implications of the opening lines of 'The Vietnam Project' may be understood: 'My name is Eugene Dawn. I cannot help that. Here goes.'[11] These words stand alone, and then the opening words of the first section of the novella follow: 'Coetzee has asked me to revise my essay.'[12] The author has immediately caught the reader off guard by referring, apparently, to himself, in the third person, and the character named thus is seen as an adversarial authority figure in the troubled feelings of the conflicted narrator/writer, Dawn. His troubled feelings have to do with how he must justify and further the American war in Vietnam, but they also have to do with disorientations of selfhood which may not be amenable to simple historical or cultural narratives. These first sentences of the opening novella may be seen as a preface in just this way to the second novella also, in which a 'historical' and 'realistic' account of a journey into the lands of the South African Bushmen two hundred years earlier becomes a complex enquiry into how to present a truthful narrative of past events. The troubled narrator, 'Coetzee', an ancestor of the novelist, is shadowed by Coetzees of other generations, even including the translator, 'J. M. Coetzee', all conspiring to establish a version of the history of conquest in the Cape. Yet even in the fundamental gesture of naming fictional characters, Coetzee provokes the reader to consider the arbitrariness of conventions in fiction, and the embedded meanings in the acts of naming and describing, since the story told is always a reflection of the character and beliefs of the teller.

The two fictions in the novel have historical parallels in the reference to imperial/colonial contexts, but more fundamentally, they invent voices that register the breakdown into a loss of self in these contexts. This appears, at first, to undermine even the possibility of a reliable narrative voice, or, indeed, of a coherent narrative. Eugene Dawn's report on American propaganda in Vietnam reveals his awareness of the absence of an authoritative voice in radio broadcasts, and, indeed, his analysis is a projection of his own state and of a wider cultural condition: 'the voice which our broadcasting projects into Vietnamese homes is the voice of neither father nor brother. It is the voice of the doubting self, the voice of René Descartes driving his wedge between the self in the world and the self who contemplates that self.'[13] This is the more fundamental problem of narration and voice, of language and self-consciousness, that is central to these two fictions and will become the ground of much of Coetzee's subsequent writings.

The paradoxes of self and voice are investigated over and over in fictional characters, but it is evident that it is also central to Coetzee's understanding of his own work as artist, so that he characterized it as an 'autobiographical enterprise'. What emerged overtly in the autobiographical fictions, *Boyhood*, *Youth*, and *Summertime: A Novel*, and, indeed, equally overtly in novels such as *Elizabeth Costello* and *A Diary of a Bad Year*, casts a particular light on the first novel. After two decades of writing in various genres about his experience of living in South Africa, he prepares for the more 'private' matter of the autobiographical fictions in non-fictional pieces about self-knowledge, confession, and truth. In the Introduction to his translation of the Dutch novelist

Marcellus Emants's *A Posthumous Confession*, he refers to Rousseau as
the inaugurator of this exhaustive secular mode, but he sees Dostoevsky
as the key figure in the tradition to which he feels he belongs: 'after
Notes from Underground, Dostoevsky, with deeper insight into the
motives behind and inherent demands of the confessional mode,
would go on to write *The Idiot* and *The Possessed*, in which he would
destroy the pretensions of Rousseau and his heirs to arrive at true
self-knowledge.'[14] Yet by translating this Dutch novel and implicitly
allying himself with Dostoevsky, he makes clear that his goal as artist is
to experiment with the form of the 'secular confession' and its at once
doubting and aggrandizing narrator of the self. 'Artists have told us as
much about our inner life as psychologists ever have', he asserts,[15] and
in another remark about Emants, he reveals his hand: 'Emants comes to
his material in the traditional way, via chance, memory and introspection.'[16] While Coetzee's writing life is anchored in his South African
circumstances, it is evident that as an artist and truth-teller, he sees
himself in a broader European cultural context. His deeply rooted philosophical and ethical concerns are refined in terms of that European
context, but as an artist, autobiographical material is repeatedly sub-
jected to an experimental and far-reaching play to discover truths of
the inner life.[17] To understand his breakthrough as an artist, works like
Boyhood and *Youth* are key sources, not because autobiographical episodes of the two decades before Coetzee wrote *Dusklands* can be ver-
ified through biographical research but because they allow the reader
to follow the kinds of investigations into the inner life of the protagonist, named John in both volumes, which Coetzee retrospectively
identifies as the imperative of his emergence as an artist.

~

The two novellas of *Dusklands* are complementary in myriad ways, but
in beginning to understand their composition at the end of an intense
decade of searching for a role as writer, Coetzee's biographical circumstances may be outlined. In December 1961, he left South Africa for
London with the ambition of becoming a writer, a poet, and at this
stage, his mentors were Ezra Pound and T. S. Eliot, although the fiction
of Ford Madox Ford had caught his attention, and he wrote a long
thesis on Ford for his MA degree. In addition to literature, Coetzee
had taken a degree in mathematics, and in Britain, he worked for three
years as a computer programmer. His commitment to the Campaign
for Nuclear Disarmament was at odds with his research work for IBM,

whereas his metropolitan literary orientation and his desire to leave behind Cape Town appear to have come into conflict with his sudden recognition of a deep interest in his culture of origin. This was sparked by William Burchell's *Travels in the Interior of Southern Africa*, published in 1822, a memoir that documents in great detail indigenous life in the Karoo, a region inland from Cape Town which Coetzee had known intimately since childhood, 'his country, the country of his heart'. *Youth* goes on to remark of 'John' that

> ...he would like to do it: write a book as convincing as Burchell's.... The difficult part will be to give to the whole that aura that will get it onto the shelves and thus into the history of the world: the aura of truth.... Before he can bring that off, he will need to know less than he knows now; he will need to forget things. Yet before he can forget he will have to know what to forget; before he can know less, he will have to know more.[18]

This insight in *Youth* distils the experience of Coetzee during the apprenticeship phase, which lasted for almost a decade, and, of course, it highlights Coetzee's life-long scrupulousness about what may be endorsed as knowledge and truth.

At the University of Texas, where Coetzee was a graduate student for three years, 1965–68, this interest in how to write about his place of origin deepened through a more extensive reading of European explorers' narratives and also through a study of African languages in the context of structural anthropology, such as the work of Claude Lévi-Strauss, and the linguistic theories of generative grammarians such as Noam Chomsky. The intellectual foundations for Coetzee's egalitarian approach to indigenous cultures and his antipathy to imperial power were grounded in these studies. It may be that Chomsky's other role, his fierce opposition to American participation in the Vietnam war, and especially the collaboration of academics in justifying it and preparing research projects and strategies to support imperial power, drew Coetzee into an active resistance to the war and, later, to imagining the character of Eugene Dawn in 'The Vietnam Project'. In this sense, ideas for the two fictions of imperial agents may have matured simultaneously, although one must always remember his later reflections on this period: 'Nothing one picks up from generative linguistics or from other forms of structuralism helps one to put together a novel'; and 'truth is something that comes in the process of writing or comes from the process of writing'.[19] When Coetzee's student residency in Texas ended, he was allowed to stay on in the United States and to begin teaching literature at the University of Buffalo, 1968–71, but his anti-war activities with other faculty members led to his arrest, and his residency in the United States ended with his return to Cape Town in mid-1971.

His interest in writing a fiction similar to 'The Narrative of Jacobus Coetzee' originated, then, in his reading of William Burchell's memoir, and he began to assemble the materials, 'from as early as 1962'.[20] This 'reading and making notes' continued for almost a decade, and it was only on 1 January 1970 that he allowed himself to begin in earnest, surely a date chosen with deliberation. 'I wrote nothing of substance before I was thirty', he told David Attwell.

> As I remember those days [of the 1960s], it was with a continual feeling of self-betrayal that I did not write. . . . Nausea: the nausea of facing the empty page, the nausea of writing without conviction, without desire. . . . I knew that once I had truly begun, I would have to go through with the thing to the end. . . . I hesitated through the 1960s because I suspected, rightly, that I would not be able to carry it through.[21]

The writing of a first, handwritten, draft of 'a memoir of a kind that went on growing' continued for a year, and then between January and August 1971, he left it aside. In the latter month he began to prepare a typed draft, and, with revisions, this appears to have occupied him to the end of 1971. It appears, then, that in exactly two years he had brought the manuscript to near completion. In print, it is seventy pages long. After a pause of four months, he began to sketch out another fiction, 'Lies', in May 1972. He returned to it, now 'The Vietnam Project', between December 1972 and April 1973. Then, in April–May 1973, he prepared a final handwritten draft, so that this second fiction was written over a period of a year. It is forty-nine pages long. *Dusklands* is, then, a brief, highly compressed work of fiction in two parts. It was written over three and a half years, at a time of great disruption in Coetzee's life, the fiction of colonial Africa largely written while he was resident in the United States, the fiction of America written after he returned to South Africa, but in fact both fictions are remarkably similar in vision and in their ways of defining his first step into a characteristic method.

It is evident that Coetzee's preparation for writing fiction, for his definitive first work, included wide reading in European literature and philosophy. It also included serious thinking about the meaning of his

own experience in South Africa and the articulation of a profound
need for a sincere and authentic voice that would be unmistakably his
own. His experiments in the philosophy and anthropology of languages struck him later as odd 'for someone with literary ambitions,
albeit the vaguest—ambitions to speak one day in his own voice'.[22]
Rather than being a voice of authority, of certainty and of power, 'his
own voice' would express uncertainty and doubt about his own ances-
tral cultural identity and about his inheritance of a literary and spiritual
discourse. In such self-consciousness, in exploring the underpinnings
of self-consciousness, and of the notion of selfhood, Coetzee's fictional
voice and medium were established in constantly experimental terms,
but in fact there are ways in which a drama is created between the
voices of authority and 'countervoices', between a sense of an author
as an articulated and authentic presence and those sceptical procedures
that free dimensions of the self scarcely amenable to articulation,
except perhaps in art. 'Writing is not free expression,' he has said. 'It is
some measure of a writer's seriousness whether he does evoke/invoke
those countervoices in himself.'[23] Indeed, it might be said that beginning with *Dusklands* and continuing into *In the Heart of the Country*
and subsequent novels, the first-person narrators embody just this radical drama between voices, and, later, in different ways, it is these felt
'countervoices' that are central and yet obliquely related to the whole
'autobiographical writing enterprise'.[24]

～

Writing is a deeply moral activity for Coetzee, and indeed the committed intellectual life that informs it. For almost ten years before he
began to write *Dusklands*, he deepened his understanding of how literature might or might not articulate an authentic selfhood and how
narrative might or might not be a medium in which the self's place in
history could be understood. Speaking to David Attwell, he remarked:
'History may be, as you call it, a process for representation, but to me
it feels more like a *force* for representation, and in that sense, yes, it is
unrepresentable.'[25] In talking about Zbigniew Herbert, a poet Coetzee
esteems highly, he recalls Herbert's thinking in a way that suggests
agreement with him: 'Herbert doesn't talk about History, but he does
talk about the barbarian, the spirit of the barbarian (embodied in such
people as Stalin), which is pretty much the same thing as history-the-
unrepresentable. Herbert's strength is that he has something to oppose
to the barbarian.'[26] This moral category of 'the spirit of the barbarian'

was known to Coetzee personally in his upbringing in South Africa; it is something he has lasting feelings about, and they are at the heart of *Dusklands*. His work might be seen as a search for 'something to oppose to the barbarian', and that search is intimately associated with the recognition of an authentic personal voice. Expressing a deep admiration for Herbert, whose work he had first read in London, he remarks: 'What one learns from Herbert is not a body of ideas but a certain style, hard, durable: a style that is also an approach to the world and to experience, political experience included.... A style, an attitude to the world, as it soaks in, becomes part of the personality, part of the self, ultimately indistinguishable from the self.'[27] In the first novel's dramatization of barbarism and psychic imprisonment, however, there is less a clarification of that voice of opposition than a yearning for it.

Coetzee's concern with language and the novel is a search for ways of recognizing and resisting complicity with barbarism. This concern could be grounded only in his earliest experience of growing up in an Afrikaans community. When he left Cape Town for London in December 1961, it was with the intention of leaving his past behind, but, to his surprise, that past returned to him in the metropolis. Although *Youth* is an autobiographical fiction, written three decades later, there is a passage that is suggestive of what happened. 'John' has the ambition to be a poet, but at a certain point he stops writing poetry and turns to prose. 'The story that emerges from the experiment, if that is what it is, a story, has no real plot. Everything of importance happens in the mind of the narrator, a nameless young man all too like himself.'[28] Unlike poetry, in which 'the action can take place everywhere and nowhere', prose 'seems naggingly to demand a specific setting' and, to his dismay and disquiet, he has set the story in South Africa: 'he would prefer to leave his South African self behind as he had left South Africa itself behind'.[29] In spite of the intention that underlay Coetzee's migration to London, he realizes that his 'South African self', rooted in a specific place, is close to the heart of his maturing imagination. The well-documented discovery of Burchell's *Travels* clearly triggered interests that went wider than the historical or narrative ones that are overtly at play in 'The Narrative' and concerns having to do with imperialism and colonization. Those interests were, to begin with, of an academic nature, and were elaborated in linguistic and philosophical terms, but it is evident that in attempting to incorporate his own most intimate childhood experiences in his understanding of the art he must create, the autobiographical underpinnings of his fiction were revealed to him early and are integral to *Dusklands* and the later fiction.

Although *Boyhood: Scenes from Provincial Life*, published in 1997, is a third-person narrative, John is the central consciousness for everything that is narrated, and if his identity as boy is the memoir's subject and is fully grounded in the startling intimacy of the details, his older novelistic self can also be sensed in the preoccupation with language and expression, with the medium of this art. John is always fighting back; he refuses to be a victim of the aggression of others, yet, at his age and degree of familial dependence, this independence is largely a private state of critical detachment. Becoming an impostor, 'another person', John registers and articulates felt complexities of violence and desire, and so the identity of the writer/narrator as impostor, and narrative as 'forgery', appear here as the strategies for truth-telling which were first adapted in *Dusklands* and in many later fictions. The aesthetic principles that guide this work are embedded in the experience of John presented in this memoir, and we must assume that the appropriate way to read *Youth* is less as autobiography than as a portrait of the artist as a young man.

John's mother and father were raised speaking Afrikaans, in rural backwaters, and continued to speak Afrikaans to their families, yet they decided that he would grow up speaking English. They spoke English in the home and sent their son to English schools; in fact, one of John's worries was that because he bore an Afrikaner name, he might be obliged to attend school in Afrikaans. It appears that he did not begin to speak the language until he was about four, but having English as his mother tongue and having a heightened consciousness of the other language, and its social and historical ramifications, led to some of the boy's most complex feelings about his cultural identity. While he had to constantly negotiate both passing contacts and more established relationships with coloured people (there are almost no blacks at all in his English/Afrikaner environment), it is his relationship to Afrikaner culture, and especially to stereotypical male behaviour, that shapes the central issues of cultural identity for him.

Male Afrikaner culture is characterized from the beginning as endemically violent. In chapter two, the secret he keeps from his mother is the violence of the school, the daily beatings by teachers, male and female, and the initiation rituals imposed by the other boys. John stands out for academic excellence and so avoids the floggings by teachers, but his sense of his own difference, his softness, instils a kind of shame. The violation and its acceptance are a sign of some obscure public honour, whereas in John's observation of them, his sense of the privacy of physical sensation becomes an obscure and troubling aspect of his individuality. There is a suggestion that the normalizing violence is a kind of rape, with life and death significance: 'If it ever happens that he is called out to be beaten, there will be so humiliating a scene that he will never again be able to go back to school; in the end there will be no way out but to kill himself.'[30] The 'scene' that he imagines is his refusal to be beaten, and the power that will allow him to refuse is rooted in a feeling of shame.

The strange thing is, it will only take one beating to break the spell of terror that has him in its grip. He is well aware of this: if, somehow, he can be rushed through the beating before he has had time to turn to stone and resist, if the violation of his body can be achieved quickly, by force, he will be able to come out on the other side a normal boy.[31]

This awareness is, perhaps, the closest he comes to a recognition of barbarism: that rape is a necessary, normalizing process in this culture. He blames his mother for making him a sissy and abnormal, for his father and his uncles all seem to have been normalized by such beatings, and so the secret he keeps from his mother is the ground of his rejection of her.

While the wish to be normal occupies John daily, far more emphatic is a recognition of his separateness and a determination to preserve that separateness, from mother, from father, and from the surrounding society and its culture. So complex are the conflicting loyalties he feels, between mother and father, home and school, 'English' and 'Afrikaner' culture, that he withdraws and creates a double life: 'By living this double life he has created for himself a burden of imposture.'[32] And yet it seems that he has no doubt that his becoming an impostor preserves a great measure of his freedom and his desires.

Language and expression are at the heart of those issues because they are the medium through which his sense of his own male body, his bond to and independence from his mother and the enveloping Afrikaner culture are brought into consciousness. As he registers the nuances of communication and meaning, the enigmatic textures of words, the abrupt revelations of estrangement, his effort to find clarity

draws recurring attention to his isolation and difference. 'Because
they speak English at home, because he always comes first in English
at school, he thinks of himself as English. . . . The range of Afrikaans he
commands is thin and bodiless; there is a whole dense world of slang
and allusion commanded by real Afrikaans boys—of which obscenity
is only a part to which he has no access.'[33] Yet on the farm of his
father's family, where a large gathering of brothers, wives, and cousins
assemble regularly, speaking Afrikaans, a dramatic change had happened
on his first visit when, playing with coloured boys, he realized he could
speak some Afrikaans. Something vital from that time remained: 'When
he speaks Afrikaans all the complications of life seem suddenly to fall
away. Afrikaans is like a ghostly envelope that accompanies him everywhere, that he is free to slip into, becoming at once another person,
simpler, gayer, lighter in his tread.'[34] In spite of this, he fears the larger
Afrikaner identity associated with his father: 'It centres just as much
on being beaten and on nakedness, on bodily functions performed in
front of other boys, on an animal indifference to privacy. . . . It is like
being sent to prison, to a life without privacy.'[35] He senses that his
father's family blame his mother for making him 'English', and he does
not understand why they 'dislike England'. Unaware of the Boer war,
for it is not taught in school History classes, he is inclined to revere
heroic and jingoistic aspects of the Empire, especially in the light of
Dunkirk and the Battle of Britain. But he knows that he is not 'truly
English'; for that there are 'tests to face, some of which he knows he
will not pass'. And so, while he feels that he 'commands with ease' the
English language, all the cultural and historical complexities in which
his feelings about himself are entangled leave him isolated and anxious
about where he really belongs. What he does undoubtedly know is
that he is an outsider and alone—except perhaps for his mother—in
his awareness of how an individual life is crushed in ritualized and
culturally sanctioned ways.

～

Most critics of Coetzee's work are focused on its political dimensions
in the light of South African circumstances, although in the first two
decades of his career, on a number of occasions, he affirmed that he did
not see it as his role to be *engagé* in the political struggle. Yet there is no
doubt that he was committed from the beginning to understanding the
truth and injustice of colonial power and how an individual might be
complicit. Dominic Head's emphasis in discussing *Dusklands* seems

just: 'complicity is a theme of the novel, and is inevitably enacted in the sequence of first-person narratives, where each narrating subject is exposed as a product and perpetrator of colonial projects.'[36] Head associates the preoccupation with complicity and authorial power with Coetzee's metafictional strategies, and remarks: 'the author's sense of complicity is emphasized by all these Coetzees...the ancestry that implicates him in the early colonial discourse of the Cape' and 'is rendered personal for Coetzee'.[37] The novelist's insight into the nature of complicity is 'personal', however, not only in his communal and historical observations or sense of inheritance but in his early experiences of his immediate family, as the later memoir fictions make clear.

While *Boyhood* clarifies the boy's experience of barbarism and self-recognition in his South African boyhood, it also focuses on another conflicted individual, his mother. In the opening scene of *Boyhood*, John is eight, it is 1948, and the family has been exiled from Cape Town to the barren outskirts of a country town called Worcester so that the father, a non-practising lawyer, can start his new job as accounts clerk in a canning factory. His mother wishes to have a bicycle so that she can escape from her daily isolation in this new housing development. Her husband ridicules the idea, 'Women do not ride bicycles, he says. His mother remains defiant. I will not be a prisoner in this house, she says. I will be free.'[38] These words set the tone and direction of the whole narrative of *Boyhood*, for in the boy's observation of the incident, all his own deepest feelings are stirred, and he is introduced to ideas of imprisonment and freedom that will become key preoccupations in his first four novels.

At first John is confused, 'what if his father is right?', and his mother's first efforts to teach herself to cycle appear futile, so that he finds himself allied with his father: 'His heart turns against her. That evening he joins in with his father's jeering. He is well aware what a betrayal this is. Now his mother is all alone.'[39] She does succeed eventually, although she cycles when he is away at school, and so he only sees her on one occasion: 'Her hair streams in the wind. She looks young, like a girl, young and fresh and mysterious.'[40] It is a low-key epiphany, a passing vision of almost transcendent beauty—somehow opposed to the squalor of the circumstances—and depths of feeling are brought to life that appear to last to the present time of writing.

John was actually sympathetic to his mother's unhappiness, and had a sense that her life had once been very different, perhaps filled with

fore she married. The enigma of that marriage preoccupies
whole inclination is to gang up with her against his father', [41]
; occasion he has slipped into ridicule, betraying her in silent
complicity. Somehow, and he does not know why, he associated himself
with common male attitudes, and the incident seems to remain with
him because for once 'he belongs with the men'. Even though his
mother did master the bicycle, she soon gave up: 'No one says a word,
but he knows she has been defeated, put in her place, and knows that he
must bear part of the blame.'[42] His felt recognition of sexual stereotypes,
abusive power, and humiliation informs Coetzee's later understanding
and surely determines his choice of this incident for the opening chapter. 'I will make it up to her one day, he promises himself.'[43]

In fact, John has an unsentimental attitude towards his mother, which
is explored throughout the book, but here it appears that he becomes
aware of the violence inherent in the texture of his daily life. She is
'escaping towards her own desire. He does not want her to go. He does
not want her to have a desire of her own.'[44] In remembering her, it is
as if the writer is working to identify and understand, to subvert, such
violence, especially in the lives of men, and indeed in the life of the
boy himself. In these simple sentences, it is as if he has plumbed some
primal and visceral impulse to dominate which courses through intimate relationships, social intercourse, and, of course, racial relations in
the tangled history of settlement in South Africa.

'The memory does not leave him', the final paragraph of the
chapter begins, as if confirming that the present tense in which John's
boyhood is narrated remains the present tense of J. M. Coetzee as
he writes. The felt truth of this small familial event is constant and
becomes a much larger truth. The final paragraph of the book, in a
chapter that describes the boy's attendance at the funeral of his mother's Aunt Annie (John is now thirteen), concludes, 'He alone is left to
do the thinking. How will he keep them all in his head, all the books,
all the people, all the stories? And if he does not remember them, who
will?'[45] In these sentences, it appears that the writer steps in to identify
himself with John's burden, and in remembering on behalf of others, it
is as if he protests on their behalf against the inescapable limitations on
a life: of death and history, poverty and place, of the imprisonment of
narrow circumstances and roles.

These episodes in *Boyhood* suggest that while Coetzee's fiction
embraced wider and wider contexts for revealing how powerlessness

can permeate a culture and a history just as much as dominance and authority, his preoccupation with complicity is rooted in lasting feelings from childhood. Those feelings are associated with his mother and with his own felt realization of betrayal, so that the duty to make restitution might not have arisen originally from ethical considerations and a deconstruction of the imperial legacies in South Africa and worldwide.

~

'The Narrative of Jacobus Coetzee' dramatizes versions of the 'Coetzee' tradition of historical self-justification. The meticulous realism through which an eighteenth-century context and 'frontiersman' voice are created is mirrored by the equally meticulous creation of a mid-twentieth century voice of a historian–editor and his objective-seeming academic method in preparing an edition of 'The Narrative'. The editor, S. J. Coetzee, who translated the original narrative from Dutch to Afrikaans, is identified as the father of 'J. M. Coetzee', the translator into English of the original narrative and the introduction to it written in Afrikaans by his 'father'. The novelist/translator has fabricated an unreliable role for himself in the transmission of historical narrative for, of course, he adopts a 'neutral' tone in the face of the revelations in 'The Narrative' of pathological racial prejudices, violence, and casual brutality. The realistic depiction of such brutality, and, indeed, other physical sensations, is certainly shocking in its intimacy—almost pornographic—and it seems that Coetzee has deliberately juxtaposed these elements in order to engage and disorient the reader.[46] Mentalities of rationality and distance jolt against images of visceral experiences, such as pain, hunger, excretion, and disorientation.

Jacobus Coetzee is obsessed to a hallucinatory degree by the violence he inflicts and experiences. At first, in the introductory pages, the attitude of the 'frontiersman' is set out as a mentality of the arrogant conqueror. While he is matter of fact in explaining how best to shoot the Bushmen when they are armed with bow and arrows or in describing how abandoned females have been sexually used by frontiersmen, he reveals a deep-seated fear of their power and speaks of 'the blindest alley of the labyrinth of myself'[47] which encounters with them—or with Hottentots who have not had contact with Europeans—draw him into. His narrative of his travels into unexplored territories is actually an exploration of this fear, for he falls seriously ill and is at the mercy of his Hottentot servants and the 'uncivilized' Hottentots and Bushmen they meet. He survives dependence and humiliation, comes close to death, experiences their violence, and descends for a time into a state of delirium, but he does survive and returns home. A year later he undertakes a second journey with the express purpose of slaughtering his former servants who have deserted him and those among whom they have sheltered. This punitive slaughter is depicted vividly.

In this narrative of the fragile hold of the 'frontiersmen' on power and authority, and on their own sanity, Jacobus Coetzee reveals his self-righteous arrogance in the colony established by his ancestors and also the recesses of his deepest fears for himself and the survival of their colonial project. The opening paragraph introduces that fear in the context of mixed-race relationships and mentions a Dutchman who has married a Hottentot. 'Everywhere differences grow smaller as they come up and we go down.... Our children play with servants' children, and who is to say who copies whom? In hard times how can differences be maintained?'[48] They are the fears and the questions which led to the establishment of apartheid in the twentieth century, in Coetzee's childhood, but the logic that led to it is explored here. By the end of Jacobus Coetzee's adventures, he seems to have learned that he might be an insignificant presence in the history of the Hottentots, and even wonders if he has cut himself off from 'an immense world of delight' in deciding that it is 'an impenetrable world', but he quickly represses such thinking: 'God's judgment is just, irreprehensible, and incomprehensible. His mercy pays no heed to merit. I am a tool in the hands of history.'[49] On the one hand, he adopts the justification of being the agent of God's inscrutable design, but when he is inclined to consider the 'point of view' of the other culture, he is pragmatic: 'I have other things to think about.'[50] And the Introduction to the text, written by his descendant, does not hesitate to further this line of thinking: 'The commando expeditions were thus in no sense genocidal.'[51] It is the certain voice of the apartheid regime; in adopting those voices grounded in an 'authenticated' history, the novelist simultaneously establishes the reality of beliefs and behaviour and subverts them.

The authorial voice of J. M. Coetzee is hidden, at once the writer of a 'real' history and yet the puppet-master of unreliable narrative voices; their unreliability is indeed a deeper realism or historical truth.[52] But Coetzee's engagement with the material of history or of contemporary events also takes him deeper than historical narrative or what he will call the 'illusionism' of Realism, and the play with narrative voices points to this more intimate interest, in language and the self.

J. M. Coetzee's first published essay was on Samuel Beckett. It is one of a series of essays published in the 1970s as the young academic worked to establish himself in the university milieu of the United States and of South Africa, after his return there in 1971. Essays on stylistics, on literary translation, and philosophy of language reflect the interests he developed at the University of Texas and at the University of Buffalo. The scientific discourse in which he articulated an approach to understanding individual literary style grew out of the research he first honed in his graduate work on the early fiction of Samuel Beckett. The 'sensuous delight' he found in Beckett's work remained an inspiration, and these essays always reveal that below the conventional academic medium, the original and experimental imagination of Coetzee is coming to terms with the grain of other individual imaginations and with the traditions of the novel genre itself. He will later characterize the time he spent on stylistics as 'a wrong turning...a false trail...it didn't lead anywhere interesting'.[53] In spite of this, the early essays throw light on his preoccupations as he clarified his own fictional style in the writing of *Dusklands*.

Beckett's *The Unnameable* is the pivot of much in Coetzee's experimental orientation at this time, following his first excitement at *Murphy*, *Watt*, and the first two novels in the Trilogy. In particular, he is moved by the opening: 'Where now? Who now? When now? Unquestioning. I, say I. Unbelieving.' His admiration of this arresting opening, highlighting the difficulties of narrative voice, is echoed later when he identifies his first pleasure in reading *Watt*: 'just the flow of a voice telling a story, a flow continually checked by doubts and scruples, its pace fitted exactly to the pace of his own mind'.[54] Beckett's work was the subject of his doctoral thesis, written in 1968, and the central focus of his earliest essays, the first published just before the writing of *Dusklands* took off, but another, later, essay situates the concern with the opening line of any work of fiction in a wider context. It shows Coetzee's significant scepticism about what he calls the conventional 'illusionism' of the realistic novel, about language and naming—especially the self, whether narrative or authorial—and about the situating of the self in historical contexts.

If Coetzee's first inspiration came through his discovery of Beckett's early fiction and his awareness of how such problems are central to Beckett's work, he became capable of writing his own fiction by articulating an individual response to them. Philosophically, these problems of self, voice, and narration will remain unresolved through Coetzee's career, and his fictions are consciously written in their shadow in the sense that readers are always made aware of them. But as a novelist, a writer writing, Coetzee must regain confidence in what he is actually doing, and the discovery of that authorial confidence for the first time is what allowed him to write *Dusklands* and to continue his fictional oeuvre. Confidence in his role as artist, as novelist, had to be won against the presence of Beckett, his first master. The essays on Beckett, which he wrote while he was working on the fiction, acknowledge his admiration of the master, but it is also possible to glimpse his dynamic engagement with Beckett's work.

In an essay on *Murphy*, for instance, he analyses a set of sentences and concludes 'that a comic antigrammar of point of view is everywhere at work' in the novel. His elaborate method of analysis simply confirms 'one's first impression' that in the narrative there are pervasive 'violations of the principle of the separation of the three estates of author, narrator, and character'.[55] Coetzee appears to view the anarchy of narrative strategies in Beckett's first novel in a comic light, although he senses that it reflects 'an attitude of reserve towards the Novel, a reluctance to take its prescriptions seriously'.[56] In *Watt*, the second novel, he finds the same 'flippant treatment of narrative decorum',[57] but from an early appreciation of the comic anarchy in *Watt*, its rejection of 'illusionism', doubts gradually emerge.

At first he frames his consideration of *Murphy* and *Watt* in Flaubertian terms:

'Grammar and Style', wrote Beckett to a friend in 1934, 'they appear to me to have become...a mask'.... What he means by Style here is style as consolation, style as redemption, the grace of language. He is repudiating the religion of style that we find in the Flaubert of *Madame Bovary*: 'I value style first and above all, and then truth.'[58]

Coetzee's dissatisfaction with *Watt* is twofold, its lack of 'external attachments' and the incoherence in its close: 'The formal and narrative indecisiveness of its ending...have caused considerable unease to me.'[59] In spite of his life-long admiration of Beckett's work, such discomfort traces the direction in which his own fiction will grow, away from Beckett, and as Beckett's career developed, the difficulties in relation to voice and narrative became more problematic for Coetzee. Radical doubt about the novel genre itself 'grows, and by the time of

The Unnameable (1953) [it] has become, in a fundamental sense the subject of Beckett's work. *The Unnameable* as a name is a token of an inability to attain the separation of creator and creation, namer and named, with which the act of creating, naming, begins.'[60] It is evident that Coetzee wants to maintain a faith in the potential of the novel to incorporate philosophical and psychological anxiety to an extreme degree and yet remain an authentic artistic medium.

The opening sentence of 'The Vietnam Project' appears to be a clear statement of independence from 'the subject of Beckett's work' and its stylization: 'My name is Eugene Dawn. I cannot help that.' But if Beckett's *Trilogy* settles into a stylization, 'an incapacity to affirm and an inability to be silent', by the late 1960s the short pieces, such as *Lessness*, have reached a terminus. Coetzee thinks of the work after *The Unnameable* as not only an embodiment of doubt, but, more significantly for him, the voices are post-mortem, 'disembodied'.[61] In brief, Coetzee wishes to maintain the fundamental rootedness of the novel in its attachments to the living world beyond the mind or the solitary voice, and in confronting the Cartesian dualism, he wants to root the voice of narrative in the reality of the body, the living, suffering body: 'I am still interested in how the voice moves the body, moves in the body.'[62] He is speaking in 1990 here, but he might have been describing *Dusklands* or *In the Heart of the Country*, both fictions in which the physicality of sensations and feelings which are rooted in them are intensely realized.

Looking back years later to the decade of immersion in Beckett's work, the graduate school years and the years of the academic articles, Coetzee commented: 'The essays I wrote on Beckett's style aren't only academic exercises in the colloquial sense of that word. They are also attempts to get closer to a secret, a secret of Beckett's that I wanted to make my own. And discard, eventually, as it is with influences.'[63] He goes on to say in this interview with David Attwell that 'it is unlikely that Beckett would have gripped me if there hadn't been in him that unbroken concern with rationality, that string of leading men savagely or crazily pushing reason beyond its limits.' This appears to describe precisely the condition of both Jacobus Coetzee and Eugene Dawn, and yet Coetzee unconvincingly protests: '*Dusklands* didn't emerge from a reading of Beckett.' 'Anti-illusionism,' he opined, by which he meant post-modernism, 'is, I suspect, only a marking of time, a phase of recuperation, in the history of the novel. The question is, what next?'[64]

Coetzee's own fiction began early, with *Dusklands*, that work of recuperation and recovery after Beckett's subversion of the tradition of fictional realism, although it becomes evident that he sees Beckett as a figure in a tradition that includes classics of confessional literature, from Augustine and Rousseau, in addition to dramatizations of confession such as Dostoevsky's *Notes from Underground*, and metafictional classics such as *Don Quixote* and *Tristram Shandy*. It is also evident that during the American years, he was exposed to the experimental fictions of Nabokov and Borges, not to forget the fiction of his colleague at the University of Buffalo, John Barth, and their example may have encouraged him in the writing of *Dusklands*. Deeply schooled in classics of European literature, however, Coetzee was compelled to test their vision and their styles against his own experience in South Africa and the United States as a prerequisite to his work of restoration of vitality to literary language and to the novel.

〜

While the naming of 'J. M. Coetzee' as the 'translator' of the documents that make up 'The Narrative of Jacobus Coetzee' may appear to be a comic embellishment, the role of translator and meanings associated with translation as a literary art were of central significance in the formation of Coetzee's writing voice at this time. In fact, his dual-language inheritance of Afrikaans and English lies behind his interest in the figure of the dual-language writer Beckett and more generally in his professional interest in language learning and translation during the Texas years and later. Even more than this, he became a translator, at first of poetry, and then, starting in 1968, he began to translate from the Dutch Marcellus Emants's novel *A Posthumous Confession*. Even as he wrote 'The Narrative', he continued this work of translation. In a sense, it was his first work of fiction, and the translation of Emants and 'The Narrative' were sent out to publishers simultaneously in January 1972.[65]

'Though I have spoken English since childhood,' Coetzee notes,

I was not brought up in a culture that anyone would recognize as English. English in South Africa is what one might call a deeply entrenched foreign language; and there is a sense in which I have always approached English as a foreigner would, with a foreigner's sense of the distance between himself and it.[66]

At first, it may be that Coetzee experienced the alienation from two languages and two cultures he has written about in *Boyhood*, but by the time he settled in London, he appears to have embraced the 'foreign' nature of all languages and literatures as a positive opportunity. He has reported that he read anthologies of contemporary poetry in translation from Germany and France, took a special interest in Beckett's translations from Mexican Spanish, and was 'bowled over' by the poetry of Josef Brodsky which he heard on the BBC Third Programme.[67] Then and throughout the 1960s, he threw himself into the learning of many languages, at first European (Dutch, German, French, Spanish, Russian), and later, in Texas, he interested himself in different African languages. This interest supported his philosophical and anthropological interest in language during his graduate studies, and when he began to teach, he offered a course on literary translation.[68] But from the beginning in London, his approach to language learning was literary:

There is something physical in confronting the poem in the original, something about the words themselves, in their own brute presence, in their own order.... The original words, the poet's words, are literally irreplaceable. The only way in which they can be supplanted is for the translator to cast them out, kill them, as it were, and start again, writing the poem a second time from the inside out as his own.[69]

Bored by conventional methods of language learning, Coetzee was highly stimulated by the strangeness, the 'unique individual weight' of the particular images of the other language. 'Spanish ... came to me as a revelation, Latin brought down to earth and given body and voice.'[70] All these remarks emphasize the physicality of other languages, their sensual and aural qualities, but it is also clear that there is a sense of strangeness that can be mastered only by imprinting one's own voice on them.

What Coetzee says of reading and translating poetry from other languages, of becoming a translator, does not appear to be much different from the role of literary critic or of writer of original fiction. 'To Beckett', he writes,

English was, of course, a native language. But it was a language from which he decided, even before he settled in France, to keep a certain sceptical distance. After his early Dublin and London phase, English ceased to come naturally to him. Each word, each phrase, each idiom had to be held up, weighed, inspected, approved, before being dropped into place in the sentence.[71]

Coetzee seems to say that, as a writer, English does not come 'naturally' to him either; that his inheritance is, in some respect, foreign to him and that, as an artist, his relationship to language is akin to that of translator. A crucial step in his becoming a novelist appears to have been his training as a translator, his adoption of a role as writer that was in some sense oblique and at odds with the experience of being a native speaker.

Coetzee's biographer, J. C. Kannemeyer, argues that Emants's novel appealed to him for a major work of translation because it was in the genre of the Confession, after St Augustine, Rousseau, and Dostoevsky. But he points to the fact that Coetzee's Introduction to the novel states: 'the author is implicated in his creature's devious project to transmute the base metal of his self into gold' and that the main character undergoes 'an agonized twisting and turning to escape confrontation with the true self of his life-history'.[72] Kannemeyer remarks that the novel may remind the reader of John wandering the streets of London in *Youth*, but surely more pertinent is the resemblance to Eugene Dawn in 'The Vietnam Project', an anguished character who also has a crime to confess, but who twists and turns to avoid admission of any guilt. 'In Emants' narrator,' Kannemeyer writes, 'Coetzee had discovered something of his deepest being—in the intensity of the writing, and perhaps also in certain resemblances in character between himself and [the protagonist] Terneer, and in the fact that both he and Terneer were trapped in an unhappy marriage.'[73] Earlier the biographer had suggested an identification through 'the motif of degeneration and the crimes of the fathers, "finding whose fault I am"'.[74] It is likely that Kannemeyer's speculations are correct, but surely the way in which Coetzee applied himself to the work of translation, the way in which he found a voice in English for the Dutchman Termeer, and so made this his first literary work, is of real significance for Coetzee's confidence as a writer of the two novellas that make up *Dusklands*. And so naming himself the 'translator' in 'The Narrative' may have been easier for him than to be identified as its author, and this is a role he adopted enthusiastically in later novels too, in *Foe* and *The Master of Petersburg*, although it might be argued that it is his characteristic role in other novels too, and especially in the autobiographical fictions late in his career.

∾

Dusklands opens with 'The Vietnam Project'; it is shorter than 'The Narrative', and complete in itself, yet in many ways it introduces the reader to the preoccupations that are elaborated in the historical context of the Dutch imperial project in South Africa. In addition, it introduces the reader to a complex style of narrative ironies. The first-person narrator, Eugene Dawn, is a remarkable character study, and Coetzee uses his self-justifying monologue to investigate attitudes and beliefs that underlie genocidal violence as a part of colonial conquest. The will to exterminate the opposition and especially the rational-izations of brutality in the thinking of a contemporary specialist in 'psychological warfare', as in a Dutch explorer who convinces himself he is carrying out God's will, mark the descent from 'dusklands' into the 'heart of darkness'. The narrator registers the forces in American culture that enable and support imperial projects such as Vietnam, but Dawn is also a complex creation in conflict with himself, his efforts to repress feelings of doubt and loss of identity issuing in violence of various kinds. The irony of his name, Dawn, is evident, for in the course of his monologue, he is enveloped in a personal turbulence that mirrors the brutal maelstrom of the battlefield itself; the apparent clar-ity and poise of early pages gradually erode until the extreme control Dawn wishes to preserve yields to mental states of increasing confusion and eventual breakdown and imprisonment.

'The Vietnam Project' opens with an epigraph that highlights the pragmatic amorality of official ways of thinking about the war. Those who oppose it are understandably horrified by images of pilots 'visibly exhilarated by successful napalm bombing runs', a technocrat argues, but the adrenalin generated by unleashing such violence is necessary for their work; the pilots cannot afford to become 'excessively depressed or guilt-ridden' by reflecting on the immediate human cost of their actions.[75] And so abstraction and the dehumanization of the victims in the eyes of the perpetrators are necessary for success, but the epigraph implies that the pilots and those who plan and 'administer' the cam-paign are also victims of this dehumanization. This is Coetzee's way into a narrative that is in essence an exploration of how Dawn is both perpetrator and victim, imprisoned in this process.

The intensely conflicted and highly lucid narrator provides an inside view of his gradual breakdown, and he remains articulate to the end, challenging his doctors' diagnosis of his condition. He is curious to understand his action, and his autobiographical narrative is, to a degree, his effort to understand what led to his act of violence: 'Why should stress have driven me to a nearly fatal assault on a child I love and not to suicide, for example, or to alcohol? We are presently inves-tigating the hypothesis that my breakdown was connected with my background in warfare. I am open to this theory, as I am open to all theorizing, though I do not believe it will turn out to be the true one.'[76] In short, the psychiatrists are specialists, as he was himself, a highly qualified researcher in social psychology, but it is evident that the failure of specialists and theorizers is that they aim to solve problems by divorcing language from feeling, especially from their own most vulnerable feelings.

The truth that appears to surface in Coetzee's fiction is revealed through Dawn's accounts of his conflicts with his boss and with his wife, both projections of his bitter sense of his own failure and his inability to live with doubt. It is an insecurity about his masculinity and about his intelligence and creativity that leads him to exaggerate such aspects of his self and his presence in the world. Coetzee suggests, playfully, through naming Dawn's boss 'Coetzee', that the conflict between them is a version of father and rebellious son, of fictional character against his creator, but in fact the character named 'Coetzee' in no sense represents the attitudes of his creator. To name him thus is to challenge the reader to discover what the difference may be. And there is no doubt that implied in the fiction is a criticism of male aggression and authority, power and abstraction, repression of any moral sense or instinctive compassion, and that the author's voice is, indeed, the opposite of the voices of both Dawn and 'Coetzee'.

Using traditional techniques of realism to provoke intense emotional engagement in dramatized scenes, Coetzee also relies on a complex and unreliable point of view. He deliberately disorients the reader and uses various strategies to challenge facile interpretations and abstractions, just as the narrator's own rationalizations are uncovered through irony and satire. One section presents the narrator rewriting the introduction of his report for his boss; it is an act of professional ventriloquism as he writes in a style that he believes his boss will find acceptable, and yet his own private voice breaks into the officially sanctioned style.

The metafictional strategies that Coetzee adapts here require of the reader a complex intellectual and emotional engagement in the decoding of literary styles. In some ways, narrative voice and language are the subjects that are foregrounded in this and in the historical fiction also, for *Dusklands* as a whole reveals that it is not only finding the appropriate voice for the writing of history which interests him. Rather, it is the investigation of how a revisionist and subversive kind of writing may be developed in dialogue with classical literary traditions, especially realism. 'I have *Herzog* and *Voss*, two reputable books, a[...] Eugene Dawn remarks towards the end of 'The Vietn[...] 'and I spend many analytic hours puzzling out the tricks [...] authors perform to give to their monologues... the air of a[...] through the looking glass'.[77] Somewhat like Swift in 'A Modest Proposal', Coetzee demands of his reader a sensitivity to ironies and narrative unreliability for cross-cultural and historical readings. In his subversion of reasoning processes in language, he implies that a style may be found which in its purity will take the reader to a selfhood within and beyond cultural or historical specificity.

'The Vietnam Project' was written after Coetzee's involuntary return to South Africa, for, in spite of his opposition to the American military campaign in Vietnam, he had wished to remain in the country, or perhaps in Canada. At first, he and his family settled in the Karoo, in an abandoned farmhouse next to 'the family farm, the place on earth he has defined, imagined, constructed, as his place of origin'.[78] From this period in late 1971, Coetzee's intense response to this landscape, fusing with childhood memories, became central to many fictions, sometimes overtly as setting, as in *In the Heart of the Country*, *The Life and Times of Michael K*, and *Summertime*, but perhaps more deeply as a visionary place or state that informed the search for artistic conviction and voice. Later, he will invoke such states as tenets of his outlook, the opposite of the anguished and imprisoned selves of Eugene Dawn or Jacobus Coetzee. If he adopts a Swiftian ventriloquism to gain intimacy with such malevolent souls, his commitment to do so comes from a belief of an opposing kind, an almost utopian vision of human possibility, the 'transcendental imperative'. In contrast to their cynicism, he posits 'grace: a condition in which truth can be told clearly, without blindness'.[79] This is surely the value he ascribes to art from the earliest enthusiasm for such writers as Beckett and Herbert. 'I am someone who has intimations of freedom (as every chained prisoner has) and constructs representations—which are shadows themselves— of people slipping their chains and turning their faces to the light.... Freedom is another word for the unimaginable, says Kant, and he is right.'[80] His personal commitment is to a kind of Platonism that includes an innate awareness of such values as justice and truth, art and love, but underlying such commitment is the indelible experience of the farm as 'Eden'.

In an essay included in *White Writing*, Coetzee examines an apparently peripheral concern, the depiction of the African landscape, yet when one considers the journey into the interior in 'The Narrative', the 'heart of the country' in the next novel, and Michael K's search for 'the garden' in a war-ravaged countryside, one realizes that Coetzee wishes to ground his sense of the self in conditions that supersede the relationship of self to historical and cultural circumstances. His interest in 'the poetics of failure' in Beckett has to be placed next to other, more local, artistic resources that guided him. In a chapter entitled 'The Picturesque, the Sublime, and the South African Landscape', he writes first of William Burchell. It emerges that he was moved not only by the scientific observations that the 'botanist, ornithologist, anthropologist, natural historian' recorded on his travels in the Cape Province in 1811–13; he was moved by Burchell as a visual artist, for he 'was an accomplished amateur painter and a thoughtful observer of the South African landscape'.[81] Burchell's book includes many reproductions of paintings and drawings he made on his journey.

In the essay, Coetzee detects a dilemma that Burchell the artist faced. Trained in European styles of landscape painting, for instance, in ways of seeing relationships within a vista, or in the use of appropriate colours for the atmospheric conditions, Burchell appears to have realized that he may have been mistaken in trying to 'see' the African landscape in the same way. Coetzee speculates about Burchell's doubts: 'Are the banks of the Gariep an oasis in the African aesthetic wilderness, or is there an African species of beauty to which the eye nurtured on the European countryside, trained on European pictorial art, is blind? If the latter, is it possible for a European to acquire an African eye?'[82] His essay continues to investigate the nature of Burchell's European training and to outline how that training might not be appropriate for many elements of the landscape of the Cape. While the essay was written for an academic occasion, it is surely suggestive of the dilemma as artist that engaged Coetzee's attention from the beginning. While his urban residence and academic training throughout the 1960s allowed him to articulate such concerns, his imagination was more deeply rooted in earlier experience, and especially in the time spent in Afrikaans communities, in particular, in school, and most of all in the farm of his paternal family in the Karoo.

In *Youth*, John's excited discovery of Burchell's *Travels* in London marked a reversal of what had been a wilful and abrasive departure from home and his devotion to high modernism. His correspondence with his mother reinforces his will to embrace his exile, to make England his home, but suddenly he finds himself thinking: 'it is his country, the country of his heart, that he is reading about.... Having shaken the dust of the ugly new South Africa from his feet, is he yearning for the South Africa of the old days, when Eden was still possible?'[83] The historical fiction *Dusklands* is set in 1760 and purports to be the account of a journey by an explorer/adventurer into the lands of the Bushmen when it is really a journey inside the mind of the narrator. It is 'of the old days', but it is far from being nostalgic, for the 'true' version is an intimate confession of the savagery and violence of 'Coetzee' and an exploration of his barbaric mentality. And so it is clear that when John thinks of 'the South Africa of the old days', this is not so much a historical epoch he is recalling with yearning; it is an earlier experience of 'Eden' granted to his young self and recorded in *Boyhood* in a long central chapter.

Voëlfontein, Bird-fountain, is the farm in the Karoo on which his father grew up, and although his uncle Son inherited it, the large family of siblings have regular reunions there. Although this is his father's world, John

loves every stone of it, every blade of grass, loves the birds that give it its name, birds that as dusk falls gather in their thousands in the trees around the fountain, calling to each other, murmuring, ruffling their feathers, settling for the night. It is not conceivable that another person could love the farm as he does.[84]

In spite of his ambiguous feelings about his mother's presence at the farm—she does not feel welcomed there by her husband's family—the chapter recounts his many pleasures on these occasions, with people as with the land itself, the farmhouse, the coloured farmhands, the animals, a passionate attachment even to 'the happy slapdash mixture of English and Afrikaans that is their common tongue when they get together. He likes this funny, dancing language, with its particles that slip here and there in the sentence.'[85] It is a world apart and 'he must go to the farm because there is no place on earth he loves more or can imagine loving more. Everything that is complicated in his love for his mother is uncomplicated in his love for the farm.'[86]

Early novels such as *In the Heart of the Country* and *The Life and Times of Michael K* seem to yearn for or recover that Eden in the Karoo, and

in *Summertime*, the final volume of the *Scenes from Provincial Life*, it is
recovered once again in the recollections of John's cousin Margot
when she recounts a visit they made there together in 1974, after John's
return from America. The character Margot appears to be an elaboration of Agnes, the young cousin to whom John became very attached
in early visits in childhood years: 'She is his first cousin, therefore they
cannot fall in love and get married. In a way that is a relief: he is free
to be friends with her, to open his heart to her. But is he in love with
her nevertheless? Is this love—this easy generosity, this sense of being
understood at last, of not having to pretend?'[87] The answer to that
question appears to be given in *Summertime* when a much older John
confides in her:

What the actual words were I don't recall, but I know I was unburdening my
heart to you, telling you everything about myself, all my hopes and longings.
And all the time I was thinking, *So this is what it means to be in love!* Because—
let me confess it—I was in love with you. And ever since that day, being in love
with a woman has meant being free to say everything in my heart.[88]

The Eden in the Karoo is not simply the paradise lost of Proust, the
source of the deepest involuntary memories, but a place where in so
many ways he is 'understood at last' in his free and separate
selfhood.

This utopian vision/memory of a place in which such a liberation
becomes possible remained with Coetzee. Even if there was much that
was alienating and barbaric on the farm, something else was forged
there.

The secret and sacred word that binds him to the farm is *belong*. Out in the
veldt by himself he can breathe the word aloud: *I belong on the farm.* What he
really believes he does not utter, what he keeps to himself for fear the spell will
end, is a different form of the word: *I belong to the farm.* . . . Voëlfontein belongs
to no one. The farm is greater than any of them.[89]

It is, of course, a Tolstoyan notion, and the older Coetzee certainly
went some way in sympathizing with aspects of Tolstoy's rejection of
the world and history, but the boy feels that it is a sacred place, his
observances there are close to ritual, and his journeys there are pil-
grimages. While Coetzee as writer moved into a metropolitan and
European literary culture, and into an academic culture in the United
States, these passages suggest that from the beginning he accepted the
challenge he uncovered in Burchell: to free himself from seeing the

African landscape with an inappropriately trained eye, to imagine how he might belong there.

~

'Eliot as a man and particularly as a young man,' Coetzee declared in a lecture entitled 'What is a Classic?',

> was open to experience, both aesthetic and real-life, to the point of being suggestible and even vulnerable. His poetry is in many ways a meditation on, and a struggling with, such experiences; in the process of making them into poetry, he makes himself over into a new person. The experiences are perhaps not of the order of religious experience, but they are of the same genre.[90]

These insights into Eliot's becoming a poet and 'making himself over' have an autobiographical resonance. How is John, struggling with his own youthful experiences, to make himself over into J. M.?

The answer appears to be to recognize in himself the 'provincial', and to discover not necessarily Pound's way or Eliot's way of leaving middle America and becoming 'European' but to find his own way of approaching the centre.

> The feeling of being out of date, of having been born into too late an epoch . . . is all over Eliot's early poetry. . . . This is a not uncommon sense of the self among colonials—whom Eliot subsumes under what he calls provincials—particularly young colonials struggling to match their inherited culture to their daily experience.[91]

On familiar ground now, Coetzee continues: 'To such young people, the high culture of the metropolis may arrive in the form of powerful experiences which cannot, however, be embedded in their lives in any obvious way, and which seem therefore to have their existence in some transcendent realm. In extreme cases'—and this appears to prefigure what is explored in the drama of *Youth*—'they are led to blame their environment for not living up to art and to take up residence in an art-world. This is a provincial fate—Gustave Flaubert diagnosed it in Emma Bovary, subtitling his case study *Moeurs de province*—but particularly a colonial fate.'[92] This closing phrase appears to disclose that Coetzee may not be thinking of the canon of English literature, or English culture, but the culture of Dutch/German Protestantism and the mythologizing of that culture by the Afrikaners, a version of the 'colonial fate' written out in 'The Narrative of Jacobus Coetzee'; the high art of Europe, as interpreted for a time by Eliot and Pound may be the yearned-for but risky liberation from it.

Some years before he turned to the Eliot/Pound perspective on the 'transcendent realm' of classical European culture, Coetzee discloses that he had made a more fundamental discovery which determined his 'autobiographical path'. In the summer of 1955, when he was fifteen, Coetzee heard for the first time a recording of classical music: Bach's 'Well-Tempered Clavier', played on the harpsichord. It was an accidental event—there was no music in his family—a recording overheard from the house next door, and in spite of an initial teenage impulse to reject it because it was 'classical', he became entranced:

> I was being spoken to by the music as music had never spoken to me...after which everything changed. A moment of revelation which I will not call Eliotic—that would insult the moments of revelation celebrated in Eliot's poetry—but of the greatest significance in my life nevertheless: for the first time I was undergoing the impact of *the classic*.... The revelation in the garden was a key event in my formation.[93]

What does he mean by 'the classic'? The rest of Coetzee's lecture in 1991 is an attempt to provide a definition that takes into account his own experience of revelation, and that of Eliot. Coetzee is temperamentally sceptical of revelation-experiences and indeed of the critical evaluations of high art. 'Is being spoken to across the ages a notion that we can entertain today only in bad faith?' he asks,[94] and there is no doubt that a central preoccupation of Coetzee's whole work is 'bad faith', especially in sexual and political matters, but also in relation to artistic expression and spiritual experience.

He does not follow the 'autobiographical path' in the remainder of the lecture, but his definition of the classic is surely significant in relation to the work he undertook in his life. 'It is not the possession of some essential quality that...makes it possible for the classic to withstand the assault of barbarism. Rather, what survives the worst of barbarism, surviving because generations of people cannot afford to let go of it and therefore hold on to it at all costs—that is the classic.'[95] In Coetzee's awakening to the 'bad faith' of the Afrikaner society into which he was born, and the 'bad faith' of the literary culture that at first he was drawn to in opposition to it, an awakening too to historical relativism, he is driven to find in the notion of 'the classic' an anchor for his work. The intimations of Eden Coetzee found in Bach's music and in the innocent love and the possibility of perfect communication on the farm are integral to his art, even when, as in *Dusklands*, it dramatizes the inverse. In the opposing terms 'barbarism' and 'the classic', the beginnings of Coetzee's spiritual, moral, and literary odyssey are framed. Speaking in his public voice in that lecture, he recalls hearing the voice of Bach, and this 'revelation' is surely the beginning of what he will elsewhere call the 'transcendental imperative' in artistic creation, the discovery of a voice that will 'speak across the ages'.

∾

The paradoxes of voice and knowledge absorbed at an early age by John and explored in *Boyhood* and *Youth* mark out the imperative that shaped the work of J. M. Coetzee from *Dusklands* to later novels such as *Elizabeth Costello* and *Diary of a Bad Year*. Throughout his career, Coetzee has adopted fictional strategies to avoid any hint of an omniscient voice, but he has distinctive ways of being a constant presence in his fictions; in fact, this elusive presence is the hallmark of his complex body of fictions. Consider the ambiguous self-referential strategies that create quasi-autobiographical fictions in the second half of his career, and, earlier, in playing with known narratives, as in the life of Dostoevsky (in *The Master of Petersburg*), Robinson Crusoe (in *Foe*), and Kafka's fiction (in *The Life and Times of Michael K*). Elizabeth Costello, in the novel named after her, actually presents lectures that Coetzee himself had delivered in her name, and *Diary* includes brief essays which express ideas presented elsewhere by Coetzee in his own name. In the final volume of *Scenes from a Provincial Life*, the subject, John Coetzee, is represented as being already dead. A fictional biographer interviews people who had known him at the beginning of his career, at the time *Dusklands* was published and he was writing his second novel, *In the Heart of the Country*, and so, in effect, five different narrators create, in their own voices, five different images of John. These are briefly counterpointed with extracts from John's Notebooks and comments of the biographer. Such narrative strategies and ironic juxtaposition of voices in this 'biographical' project arise directly from the characteristic style Coetzee first invented in *Dusklands*.

In this final volume of self-portraiture, *Summertime: Fiction*, he includes an oblique account of the publication of *Dusklands*, and the book is referred to by name. Julia, a woman with whom John is having an affair, recalls that he presented her with one of two proof copies he had received. He had not previously disclosed to her that he was working on the book, and when she asks if it is fiction, he replies 'Sort of'. John tells her that the character S. J. Coetzee, the historian and the editor of the memoirs of Jacobus Coetzee, is not, indeed, his father. Julia shows little interest in either of the fictions that make up the novel or in the experimental genre he adopted, although she expresses the opinion to the biographer that she believes it is easier to invent unlikeable characters.

A further conversation ensues, however, on John's motivation for writing:

'Do you really believe that?' he said. 'That books give meaning to our lives?'

'Yes.' I said. 'A book should be an axe to chop open the frozen sea inside us. What else should it be?'

'A gesture of refusal in the face of time. A bid for immortality.' ...

'But why should the people of the future bother to read the book you write if it doesn't speak to them, if it doesn't help them to find meaning in their lives?'

'Perhaps they will still like to read books that are well written.'[96]

Youth and *Summertime*, written thirty years after the composition of Coetzee's first fictions, outline the high principles of historical truth and artistic vision that guided his work from the beginning, and yet there is a comic tone playing over this scene in *Summertime*, as in *Youth*. Julia confesses to being a pragmatist and believes that 'Principles are the stuff of comedy' because they 'bump into reality' and she acknowledges that she looked back on young John 'with affection' because she sees him as a figure of 'dour comedy'.

Julia and the other interviewees, whose recollections make up most of the book, offer limited and partial views of John as a young author in the 1970s, are largely unsympathetic to him, and indeed the comic tone arises in part from the unreliability and ambiguity of the whole biographical/fictional project. In spite of this elaborate exercise in 'forgery', Coetzee allows the reader to understand something of the convictions and ambitions that animated his first work, and indeed, it might be said that the forgery of voices, the release of countervoices, is Coetzee's most characteristic way of clarifying the self and historical truth. This he did for the first time in *Dusklands*.

In the narrative voices of Jacobus Coetzee, S. J. Coetzee, and Eugene Dawn, he creates impassioned portraits of characters who are abhorrent to him. As characters in fiction, they are as real as he can make them in their time and place; they are historically authentic, yet he simultaneously subverts that rootedness of local identity to allow the reader to experience their psychic and intellectual imprisonment. In this way, *Dusklands* implies that desire for untrammelled freedom and a purer experience of life—the desire of his mother on her bicycle, and of 'summertime' in Karoo. For Coetzee, what is 'unimaginable' or 'unrepresentable' demands all the more to be imagined and represented.

Epilogue

'Writer as writer'

The figures of V. S. Naipaul, William Trevor, Alice Munro, Mavis Gallant, and J. M. Coetzee presented themselves as subjects for this investigation as I came to the end of writing *Young John McGahern: Becoming a Novelist*. As in the case of McGahern, for decades I had followed with great pleasure their long careers as writers of fiction, and in the cases of Naipaul and Coetzee of non-fiction. They are among the most significant literary artists of the period from the 1950s into the twenty-first century; in their different ways, they have revitalized the traditions of European fictional realism. Over those long writing lives, their reputations have grown to the point of international celebration, and three of them are Nobel laureates: Naipaul, Coetzee, and Munro. I wanted to go back to their beginnings, to investigate the circumstances in which each of them had found a mature style.

I might never have begun to trace the many elements that coalesced in John McGahern's writing voice in *The Barracks* had he not spoken so enthusiastically of Proust on the first occasion I heard him read from his fiction. He spoke of Proust's essay 'Days of Reading', and then, in conversation, he identified *By Way of Sainte-Beuve* as a crucial work for him in his earliest years of apprenticeship. It came as a surprise much later to find V. S. Naipaul quoting from *By Way of Sainte-Beuve* at the opening of his Nobel address, and returning to Proust's essays at its close. Neither McGahern nor Naipaul wrote fiction that resembles *In Search of Lost Time*, but each of them drew strength from Proust's sense of the 'writer as writer and the writer as a social being'. 'I have always moved by intuition alone,' Naipaul said on the Nobel occasion, 'I have no system, literary or political. I have no guiding political idea.'[1] The validity of this claim has been debated, of course, especially when, after writing four books of fiction, he turned to non-fiction, yet the relationships between biographical provenance, public persona, authorial voice, and writer-self is a complex and centrally engaging one. In addition to Naipaul, three others, Gallant, Trevor, and Munro, have all acknowledged their rereading of Proust, and this suggests that Proust's experiment with an ambiguously autobiographical and narrative voice is close to their own sense of their presence as novelists and storytellers.

I have tried to investigate how each writer found an appropriate balance between these different selves. My focus has been narrow, and I have wanted to do justice to the definitive emergence of the writer-self. There is no new biographical documentation here, but in each case I have argued for a certain emphasis, a way of cutting through to identify the vital forces that enabled a creative self to become articulate. These are essays that use the genres of literary biography and literary criticism to achieve a kind of insight that neither alone can do. 'Writing the lines' is undoubtedly what William Trevor and the others do all day, and when we read, we too are focused on the sentences, word following word, yet overshadowing the lines or underlying them are psychic energies that are felt by writer and reader. The imaginative dilation that readers experience leads us to think of a novel or story as a screen on which the creative self of the writer is cast not only in words but in the vision that radiates through them. Or, to return to the guiding metaphor of this book, readers can easily imagine that they hear the voice of the writer echoing directly or indirectly through the narrative style. Vision and voice are, then, closely identified by the writers, and all of them bear witness to the origins of the creative achievement in memory, in images, and internalized voices.

It is not easy to situate the writing of literature in persuasive biographical contexts, and since many writers have protected their social selves from 'the paper men', it may be unwise to try.[2] Many fine literary biographies have been written, say, since Ellmann's *James Joyce*, but too often biographers have been circumstantial, presenting merely a scaffolding for the creative life, and far from convincing in their claims to cast light on the singular imagination at work or on the nature of the achievement. Yet it is this vision and voice I have tried to trace in these essays, and to detect its radiation, its resonances, at the moment of its emergence. Writers themselves are the best witnesses of this process, and Eudora Welty's *One Writer's Beginnings* strikes me as illuminating in this regard. Welty's three lectures at Harvard, later issued as a book, are entitled 'Listening', 'Learning to See', and 'Finding a Voice'. In the latter, she concludes, regarding her own self-discovery: 'Writing these stories, which eventually appeared joined together in the book called *The Golden Apples*, was an experience in a writer's own discovery of affinities.... what I do make my stories out of is the *whole* fund of my feelings, my responses to the real experiences of my own life.'[3] Welty goes on to discuss one story that was her breakthrough: 'Not in Miss Eckhart as she stands solidly and almost opaquely in the surround of her story, but in the making of her character out of my most inward and most deeply feeling self, I would say I have found my voice in my fiction.'[4] Seamus Heaney's similar emphasis on 'finding a voice' in his essay 'Feeling into Words' encouraged me at the outset to focus on how art 'mediates between the origins of feeling in memory and experience and the formal ploys that express these' in the stories and novels of the individual writers. Each essay here is distinct then because it is in the original sense an *essai* that as far as possible preserves the exploratory process of the writer's movement towards a confluence of talent, craft, and the '*whole* fund' of feeling in his or her own life.

Certain similarities are evident, and although my selection of writers who came to maturity within a twenty-year period predetermined many of these similarities, my sense of their distinct writing selves restrains me from drawing conclusions of a literary-historical nature. Beginning to write in the mid-twentieth century, in parts of the English-speaking world that had formerly been colonies in the British Empire, and conscious of the major English figures of modernism and of the post-war literary landscape, each writer nevertheless set out to discover the appropriate form and style for his or her own work. Established literary figures provided examples and inspiration, and were models for apprentice work that preceded the breakthrough achievement, but all these writers insist on their freedom to be guided by intuition in their exploration of their own material and in their discovery of their own voice.

Notes

PROLOGUE: THE WRITING VOICE

1. V. S. Naipaul, *Literary Occasions: Essays*, introduced and edited by Pankaj Mishra (New York, 2003, repr. 2004), 14.
2. *Literary Occasions*, 14–15.
3. Mira Stout, 'The Art of Fiction, CVIII: William Trevor', *The Paris Review*, 110 (Spring 1989), 110.
4. J. M. Coetzee, *Doubling the Point: Essays and Interviews*, edited by David Attwell (Boston, 1992), 53. This is the single, most valuable book for the study of J. M. Coetzee's work. Coetzee cooperated with Attwell over a two-year period in a series of extraordinarily reflective interviews about the development of his work up to 1990. Interspersed with this sequence of interviews are essays and articles written from the late 1960s to the late 1980s. Also, 'Homage', *Threepenny Review* (Spring 1993), 6.
5. Mavis Gallant, 'What is Style?' in *Paris Notebooks: Essays and Reviews* (Toronto, 1986, repr. 1988), 176.
6. *Paris Notebooks*, 179.
7. Gallant placed this phrase of Pasternak as the epigraph to her Introduction to *Home Truths: Selected Canadian Stories* (Toronto, 1981).
8. *Doubling the Point*, 246.
9. Trevor/Stout Interview, 125.
10. Alice Munro, 'What is Real?' in John Metcalfe, ed., *Making It New: Contemporary Canadian Stories* (Toronto, 1982), repr. in Metcalfe and J. R. (Tim) Struthers, eds., *How Stories Mean* (Erin, Ontario, 1993), 334.
11. Proust, quoted by Naipaul, *Literary Occasions*, 195.
12. Trevor/Stout Interview, 137.
13. Among the biographical sources I have relied on are Patrick French, *V. S. Naipaul: The World As It Is* (New York, 2008); Robert Thacker, *Alice Munro: Writing her Lives* (Toronto, 2005, rev. ed. 2011); Dolores MacKenna, *William Trevor: The Writer and His Work* (Dublin, 1999); and J. C. Kannemeyer, *J. M. Coetzee: A Life in Writing*, trans. Michiel Heyns (London, 2013). I have also made use of interviews, autobiographical essays, and reflections, and these will be cited in the appropriate places.
14. Samuel Beckett, 'Texts for Nothing, IV', in *No's Knife* (London, 1967), repr. in *The Complete Short Prose, 1929–1989*, edited by S. E. Gontarski (New York, 1995), 114.

I. V S. NAIPAUL'S *MIGUEL STREET*

1. V. S. Naipaul, *Finding the Centre: Two Narratives* (Harmondsworth, Middlesex, 1985), ix–x.

2. *Finding the Centre*, 16. These opening sentences are identical to those that appear in 'Bogart' in *Miguel Street* (Harmondsworth, Middlesex, 1971), 9.

3. *Finding the Centre*, 19.

4. V. S. Naipaul, *A Way in the World: A Sequence* (London, 1994), 27.

5. Landeg White argues in *V. S. Naipaul: A Critical Introduction* (London, 1975) that the influence of stories written by Naipaul's father is strong: 'The stories [in *Miguel Street*] thus become up-to-date and extended versions of *Gurudeva and Other Indian Tales*. Instead of a shrinking peasant community we have a city street, instead of a clash between East and West, a contrast between a small unimportant island and a world of opportunity abroad. But the antithesis remain the same' (49).

6. I have relied largely on Patrick French, *The World Is What It Is* for biographical circumstances, but the biographer does not enter into the kind of interpretation of the circumstances of composition presented here.

7. V. S. Naipaul, *A Writer's People: Ways of Looking and Feeling* (London, 2007, repr. 2008), 23.

8. *A Writer's People*, 1.

9. *Literary Occasions*, 192.

10. French, 37.

11. *A Way in the World*, 26.

12. *A Way in the World*, 83.

13. V. S. Naipaul, *The Enigma of Arrival: A Novel in Five Sections* (Harmondsworth, Middlesex, 1987), 135.

14. *The Enigma of Arrival*, 117.

15. *A Way in the World*, 83.

16. *A Way in the World*, 83.

17. *A Way in the World*, 86.

18. *A Way in the World*, 87.

19. *A Way in the World*, 95.

20. *Miguel Street*, 165.

21. *Miguel Street*, 165.

22. *Miguel Street*, 9.

23. *Miguel Street*, 9.

24. *Miguel Street*, 10.

25. *Miguel Street*, 12.

26. *Miguel Street*, 14.

27. *Miguel Street*, 160.

28. *Miguel Street*, 164–5.

29. *Finding the Centre*, 17.

30. *Finding the Centre*, 36.

31. *Finding the Centre*, 29, 72.

32. *Literary Occasions*, 14–15. The essay from which I have quoted was originally published in the *New York Review of Books* in 1999, under the title 'Reading and Writing: A Personal Account'.

33. French, 158.

34. *Finding the Centre*, 36–7.

35. *Finding the Centre*, 39.

36. In a Foreword to an edition of his father's stories reprinted by André Deutsch in 1975, Naipaul wrote of the singular importance of Henry Swanzy and 'Caribbean Voices' to his father and himself. The 'Foreword to *The Adventures of Gurudeva*' is included in *Literary Occasions*.

37. *A Writer's People*, 2.

38. V. S. Naipaul, *The Middle Passage* (Harmondsworth, Middlesex, 1969), 42.

39. *Literary Occasions*, 113, 125, and 121.

40. Diana Athill, *Stet: A Memoir* (London, 2000), 206.

41. *Stet*, 206.

42. *A Way in the World*, 86–7.

43. V. S. Naipaul, *Half a Life* (New York, 2001), 79.

44. *Half a Life*, 80.

45. Bruce King, *V. S. Naipaul*, 2nd edn. (London, 2003), 32.

46. *Literary Occasions*, 192.

47. King, 32. Londeg White concludes a consideration of *Cannery Row* as a model as follows: '*Cannery Row* can have given Naipaul little help with his first and most basic problem, namely, how to do justice to a society one has by choice left behind' (51). But White does not consider Joyce as a model, whose challenge in exile was precisely this. On the other hand, even though Bruce King remarks that the stories differ from both *Cannery Row* and *Dubliners* in their 'social comedy and lightness of tone', he observes that 'the narration does not romanticize, sentimentalize or protest' and continues: 'Naipaul binds together the narrative and the prose by repetitions of sounds, words, phrases, sentence patterns, images, parallel and analogous events. What seems simple and easy, almost natural story telling, will be found to be highly crafted towards continuity, movement and the symbolic' (25).

48. V. S. Naipaul, *Between Father and Son: Family Letters*, edited by Gillon Aitken (New York, 2001), 10; 257.

49. *The Middle Passage*, 42.

50. Bruce King's discussions of, for instance, *The Mimic Men* and *The Enigma of Arrival* are remarkable for his placing of these works in modernist traditions. Regarding the former, King concludes: 'Naipaul had become like Singh an uprooted colonial, a permanent homeless exile, wedded to his writing and his desk, seemingly writing about the upheavals and turmoils of the colonial and postcolonial world, but in actuality giving order to his own life through writing.... It is a Caribbean East Indian rewriting *A Portrait of the Artist* and *A la recherche du temps perdu*' (73–5). And note: 'In

The Enigma of Arrival Naipaul has revised a well-known form of early modernist fiction, the autobiographical novel. The relationship of the autobiographical to the fictional is given aesthetic distance and the origins of the novel are explained by the autobiographical. Characteristics shared by *Enigma* with modernist autobiographical novels by Proust, Mann and Joyce include...' (139); King's list of common elements is long and his argument convincing that, in spite of Naipaul's way of situating his work through his own critical writing, the work may be seen as a development of modernist and postmodernist aesthetics.

51. *Literary Occasions*, 191.
52. *The Enigma of Arrival*, 135–6.
53. *The Enigma of Arrival*, 136.
54. *Literary Occasions*, 15.
55. *Literary Occasions*, 20.
56. *Literary Occasions*, 194.
57. *The Mimic Men*, 251.
58. *Literary Occasions*, 193.
59. *Literary Occasions*, 193.
60. *Literary Occasions*, 182–3.
61. '*Pourquoi écrivez-vous?*' (dated by VSN Jan 25 '85), *Brick: A Literary Journal*, 49, Summer 1994.
62. Quoted in Selwyn R. Cudjoe, *V. S. Naipaul: A Materialist Reading* (Amherst, Mass., 1988), 30, from *The Times* (London), 1 February 1964.

2. ALICE MUNRO'S *DANCE OF THE HAPPY SHADES*

1. *Lives of Girls and Women* was first published in 1971 in Toronto, and in New York in 1972. It was published in the UK in 1974. *Dance of the Happy Shades* was first published in Toronto in 1968, in New York in 1973, and in London in 1973.
2. The phrase is taken from a letter by Munro to her editor, and is quoted by Robert Thacker in *Alice Munro: Writing her Lives*, 218. I have relied on Thacker for biographical detail, as well as on the brief work, Catherine Sheldrick Ross, *Alice Munro: A Double Life* (Toronto, 1992), but interviews with Munro, in spite of her disclaimers, have proved to be an invaluable source for getting close to her distinctive sense of how her work evolved.
3. Jeanne McCulloch and Mona Simpson, 'Alice Munro: The Art of Fiction CXXXVII', *Paris Review*, 131 (Summer 1994), 237. Munro also comments, speaking of her early admiration of Southern American women writers: 'There was a feeling that women could write about the freakish, the marginal ... I came to feel that was our territory, whereas the mainstream big novel about real life was men's territory' (255). She has offered another explanation for her failure to write a conventional novel: 'I have all these

disconnected realities in my own life, and I see them in other people's lives. That was one of the problems—why I couldn't write novels, I never saw things hanging together any too well' (257).

4. Thacker's lengthy biography provides much documentation on the circumstances in which Munro's work was created and brought to publication, and its critical reception, but it lacks a sense of how her aesthetic orientation emerged and was embodied in her fiction. W. R. Martin's study, *Alice Munro: Paradox and Parallel* (Edmonton, 1987) is a fine exploration of her aesthetic development from her earliest stories right through each collection up to the time of writing. His close reading of the key stories concentrates on the orientation suggested in his title, but he deliberately excludes any biographical exploration of how her art interprets her life experience.

5. Thacker, 67. Also, *The Alice Munro Papers: First Accession*, edited by Apollonia Steele and Jean F. Tenner. Biocritical essay by Thomas E. Tausky (Calgary, 1986).

6. Catherine Sheldrick Ross, 'Interview with Alice Munro', *Canadian Children's Literature*, 53 (1989), 14–24, quoted in Coral Ann Howells, *Alice Munro* (Manchester and New York, 1998), 8.

7. J. R. (Tim) Struthers, 'The Real Material: An Interview with Alice Munro', *Probable Fictions: Alice Munro's Narrative Acts*, edited by Louis K. MacKendrick (Toronto, 1983), 5. Elsewhere, Munro has spoken of Edward Hopper's paintings 'Early Sunday Morning' and 'The Barber Shop': 'These do to me exactly the same thing that the writing I respond to does and that I would like to do.' John Metcalf, 'Interview with Alice Munro', *Journal of Canadian Fiction*, 1, 4 (Fall 1972), 58.

8. *Lives of Girls*, 21–2.

9. *Something I've Been Meaning to Tell You* (Toronto, 1974, repr. 1975), 161.

10. Munro/Struthers Interview, 24.

11. *Something*, 197.

12. 'An Open Letter', *Jubilee*, 1 (1974), quoted in Thacker, 49–50.

13. *Eleven Canadian Novelists interviewed by Graeme Gibson* (Toronto, 1973), 246.

14. 'Working for a Living', *Grand Street*, 1, 1 (1981), included in *The View from Castle Rock* (New York, 2006).

15. 'She valued material things that would make your life comfortable and would remove your life from all this physical mess that we always had to confront.' Munro/Ross Interview, quoted in Ross, 33.

16. Eleanor Wachtel, 'An Interview with Alice Munro', *The Brick Reader*, edited by Linda Spalding and Michael Ondaatje (Toronto, 1991), 289.

17. *Who Do You Think You Are?*, a title which reflects Munro's concern with her exiled condition, and the judgement of a small town community, was published outside Canada with the title *The Beggar Maid*.

18. Munro/Gibson Interview, 248–9.

19. Munro/Gibson Interview, 256.

20. Munro/Gibson Interview, 241.
21. W. R. Martin has considered certain similarities between Munro and Joyce and traced some indebtedness. 'Alice Munro and James Joyce', *Journal of Canadian Fiction*, 2 (1979), 120–6.
22. L. M. Montgomery, *Emily of New Moon*, with an Afterword by Alice Munro (Toronto, 1923, repr. 1989), 9.
23. All quotations in this paragraph from Montgomery, 357–8.
24. Quotations in this paragraph from Montgomery, 359.
25. Montgomery, 360.
26. Harold Horwood, 'Interview with Alice Munro', *The Art of Alice Munro: Saying the Unsayable*, edited by Judith Miller (Waterloo, Ontario, 1984), 124.
27. In addition to O'Connor's stories in the *New Yorker*, Munro has expressed admiration for Mary Lavin and Maeve Brennan, two other Irish writers of stories who appeared regularly in the magazine in the 1950s and 1960s. Indeed, it may be that her interest in Lavin's work, in Irish writing, and in the personal voice as a characteristic element of short fiction was more focused by O'Connor's highly regarded *The Lonely Voice: A Study of the Short Story* (New York, 1963).
28. See Munro/Struthers Interview, 14–15, for a discussion of the difference between reading as a reader and reading as a writer, and Munro's preference for remaining unconscious of which writer's work may be an actual influence. Munro also remarked in this interview on the difference between a 'real story' and an 'exercise' or an 'imitation', 20–1.
29. Alice Munro, 'Golden Apples', *The Georgia Review*, 53, 1 (Spring 1999), 22–4. Quotations in this and the following paragraphs are from this brief tribute to Welty's work.
30. Thacker, 141–2.
31. Munro/Gibson Interview, 243.
32. See Munro/Struthers Interview, 6–7. In *Figuring Grief: Gallant, Munro, and the Poetics of Elegy* (Montreal and Kingston, 1992), Karen E. Smythe remarks that Agee's realism 'both portrays and embodies a psychology of grieving' (112).
33. Munro/Struthers Interview, 21.
34. *Happy Shades*, 190.
35. *Happy Shades*, 194.
36. *Happy Shades*, 191.
37. *Happy Shades*, 198–9.
38. *Happy Shades*, 202.
39. Thacker, 73.
40. Munro/Gibson Interview, 258. Smythe comments: 'Life is turned not so much into pure "art"…but life and grief become *story*—yet another *version* of life, but a mysterious, legendary, and mythological version rather than an historical one. The lines between art and life are questioned by Munro' (112).

41. Sheila Munro reports that 'my mother told me that in her early twenties she wanted to write like Virginia Woolf or Henry James.' *Lives of Mothers and Daughters: Growing Up with Alice Munro* (Toronto, 2001), 37.
42. *How Stories Mean*, 332.
43. *Lives of Girls*, 31.
44. Munro/McCulloch and Simpson Interview, 237.
45. This opening scene includes echoes of the opening scene of Agee's *A Death in the Family*.
46. *Happy Shades*, 2.
47. 'I was reading Proust all the time I was writing *Lives of Girls and Women*— [laughter] reading him mostly for encouragement because I used to worry about going into too much detail about things, then I would go and read several pages of Proust.... There's an enormous reassurance there that anything is worth one's attention and that everything is worth attention.' Munro/Struthers Interview, 14. One need not limit her reading of Proust to the actual year of writing *Lives of Girls*, for she has said that she was drawing on the work of the previous five years.
48. *Happy Shades*, 3.
49. *Happy Shades*, 4–6.
50. *Happy Shades*, 7.
51. *Happy Shades*, 12.
52. *Happy Shades*, 14.
53. *Happy Shades*, 16.
54. *Happy Shades*, 17.
55. *Happy Shades*, 18.
56. Alice Munro, 'The Colonel's Hash Resettled', in John Metcalf, ed., *The Narrative Voice: Short Stories and Reflections by Canadian Authors* (Toronto, 1972), repr. in *How Stories Mean*, 190.
57. *Happy Shades*, 35.
58. *Happy Shades*, 31–3.
59. *Happy Shades*, 36–8.
60. *Happy Shades*, 42–3. 'The tension between fact and fiction is explored by the first person narrator of "Images". This fiction-elegy might be described as an achronological memoir.' Smythe, 113.
61. Q: 'Have your sense of identity and your attitude towards the twenty years that you spent in Vancouver and Victoria changed?' AM: 'Well, it's probably coming out in that I now have a very strong sense of wanting to write about that time and seeing it in that distant, set-off, special way that I used to see Ontario when I lived in Vancouver and Victoria.' Munro/Struthers Interview, 32–3.
62. *Something*, 197.
63. 'Home', *New Canadian Stories* (Ottawa, 1974), repr. *The View from Castle Rock* (Toronto, 2006), 288–91.
64. *The View from Castle Rock*, x.

65. *The View from Castle Rock*, x.
66. *Dear Life* (Toronto, 2012), 319.
67. *Dear Life*, 284.

3. WILLIAM TREVOR'S *MRS ECKDORF IN O'NEILL'S HOTEL*

1. Trevor/Stout Interview, 125. This interview is the single most important source for Trevor's comments on his work, and, indeed, the writer confirmed that it was seen by him and revised before publication and that in his mind it has a definitive status. See 'An Interview with William Trevor Conducted by Tom Adair', *Linen Hall Review*, 11, 3 (Winter 1994), 4–8. I have also relied on other interviews and on Dolores MacKenna, *William Trevor: The Writer and His Work* for biographical information regarding the early decades of Trevor's career.
2. *A Standard of Behaviour* (London, 1958) was followed by *The Old Boys* (London, 1964), *The Boarding House* (London, 1965), *The Love Department* (London, 1966), and *Mrs Eckdorf in O'Neill's Hotel* (London, 1969). The first volume of stories was *The Day We Got Drunk on Cake and Other Stories* (London, 1967).
3. John Banville, 'Relics': review of *Two Lives: Reading Turgenev and The House in Umbria*. *New York Review of Books*, 26 September 1991, 29–31, repr. in Suzanne Morrow Paulson, *William Trevor: A Study of the Short Fiction* (New York, 1993), 166–7.
4. Mark Ralph-Bowman, 'William Trevor' (Interview), *Transatlantic Review*, 53/54 (1976), 12.
5. Trevor/Stout Interview, 143–4.
6. Gregory A. Schirmer, *William Trevor: A Study of his Fiction* (London, 1990), 38–9. Trevor's remark is in the interview with Ralph-Bowman, 8.
7. MacKenna, 230.
8. Trevor/Stout Interview, 149.
9. I have accepted Trevor's categorization of himself as a storyteller: 'The writer and the person are two very separate entities. You think as a person in a way that is not the same as the way you think as a writer. It is only when you actually feel, as a writer, "*this* has got the makings of a story in it," that you will use it. Otherwise it really has no interest to you as a writer.' Trevor/Stout Interview, 128–9.
10. Seán Dunne, 'The Old Boy', interview with William Trevor, *The Sunday Tribune*, 2 June 1985, 17; quoted in Schirmer, 3.
11. Trevor/Stout Interview, 131.
12. *Excursions in the Real World* (Toronto, 1993, repr. 1994) is a selection of reviews and articles written occasionally between 1970 and 1992 and arranged in a roughly chronological sequence.
13. 'I think it is just a kind of primitive belief in God. I think that certainly occurs in my books. I'm always saying my books are religious; nobody ever

agrees with me. I think there is a sort of God-bothering that goes on from time to time in my books.' Trevor/Stout Interview, 133. The remark on the 'purely Irish novel' is in Peter Firchow, ed., *The Writer's Place: Interviews on the Literary Situation in Contemporary Britain* (Minneapolis, 1974), 306; quoted in Schirmer, 40.

14. *Excursions*, 51.

15. MacKenna, 51.

16. MacKenna, 55.

17. Amanda Smith, 'PW Interviews William Trevor', *Publishers Weekly*, 28 October 1983, 80.

18. Trevor/Stout Interview, 125.

19. *Excursions*, 168.

20. *Excursions*, 3.

21. Trevor/Stout Interview, 143.

22. Trevor/Stout Interview, 137.

23. Trevor/Stout Interview, 135–6.

24. Gregory Schirmer focuses his central argument by invoking E. M Forster's 'Only Connect' motto in *Howards End*, and setting in opposition to it T. S. Eliot's lines from *The Waste Land*: 'On Margate Sands. / I can connect / Nothing with nothing'. Schirmer sees the poles of Trevor's imagination as compassion and relationship versus alienation and incoherence and reads many works of fiction as exemplifying the moral dilemmas that arise as characters incline towards one extreme or the other.

25. 'Assia', *Excursions*, 109–15.

26. William Trevor, ed., *The Oxford Book of Irish Short Stories* (Oxford, 1989), xiv.

27. Trevor/Stout Interview, 127. Mary Fitzgerald-Hoyt remarks that *Mrs Eckdorf in O'Neill's Hotel* is an effort to find an 'Irish voice' using Joyce as a model, but concludes that provincial Ireland rather than Dublin was his fictional terrain; in spite of this, she finds Joyce a constant presence in his work and refers to the many 'Dublin stories' in later collections. *William Trevor: Re-imagining Ireland* (Dublin, 2003). Kristen Morrison comments that *Mrs Eckdorf* 'has all the variety of Joyce's *Ulysses* and might be seen as a parody of it'. *William Trevor* (New York, 1993), 54.

28. *Excursions*, xii.

29. Morrison has noted the importance of names and suggests that Eckdorf may actually combine the German '*echt* (genuine, true, real, sincere) and *dorf* (as a card term, meaning "discard")' (115).

30. *Mrs Eckdorf in O'Neill's Hotel* (Harmondsworth, Middlesex, 1973, reissued 1982), 184.

31. Schirmer reads the novel as a character study of Mrs Eckdorf, her discovery of her own self as victim and aggressor, and her conversion to a belief in forgiveness, but in arguing that she is driven to madness by the disinterest of others in her new-found faith, he does not account for the scope of

the novel as a tapestry of different kinds of stories, moral realism being only one of them.

32. 'Lives of the Saints', a review of Brian Moore, *No Other Life*, *New York Review of Books*, 21 October 1993, 3.

33. *Mrs Eckdorf*, 20.

34. *Mrs Eckdorf*, 34.

35. *Mrs Eckdorf*, 35. Morrison has perceptive remarks on Ivy Eckdorf's photographic art, but she does not note the contrast between this modern medium and the traditional religious images, especially of the Italian Renaissance, which create a context for Mrs Sinnott.

36. *Mrs Eckdorf*, 35.

37. *Mrs Eckdorf*, 126.

38. *Mrs Eckdorf*, 128.

39. *Mrs Eckdorf*, 129.

40. *Mrs Eckdorf*, 264.

41. *Mrs Eckdorf*, 263.

42. William Trevor, *Fools of Fortune* (London, 1983, repr. 1984), 234.

43. William Shakespeare, *Henry IV*, Part One, V, 4, ll. 80–2.

44. *Fools of Fortune*, 229.

45. *Fools of Fortune*, 229.

46. *Fools of Fortune*, 238.

47. *Fools of Fortune*, 239.

48. Trevor/Stout Interview, 143.

49. Trevor/Stout Interview, 136.

50. Trevor/Stout Interview, 137.

51. *Oxford Book of Irish Short Stories*, xv.

52. *Oxford Book of Irish Short Stories*, xiv.

53. *Oxford Book of Irish Short Stories*, xv.

54. 'The short story of the 20th century has affinities with the Impressionists and the post-Impressionists. It is the art of the glimpse; it deals in echoes and reverberations; craftily it withholds information.' Trevor, 'Frank O'Connor: The Way of a Storyteller', review of *Collected Stories* by Frank O'Connor, *Book World*, *The Washington Post*, 13 September 1981, 1. See also, O'Connor, *The Lonely Voice*.

55. *Oxford Book of Irish Short Stories*, xiv.

56. Trevor/Stout Interview, 136.

57. *Oxford Book of Irish Stories*, 136–7.

58. Trevor/Stout Interview, 131–2.

59. William Trevor, *A Writer's Ireland: Landscape in Literature* (New York, 1984), 8.

60. *Excursions*, 191.

61. *Excursions*, 172–3.

62. Trevor/Stout Interview, 137.

63. *The Stories of William Trevor* (Harmondsworth, Middlesex, 1983), 185–6.

64. *Stories of William Trevor*, 185.

65. *Stories of William Trevor*, 186.

66. *Stories of William Trevor*, 187.

67. Schirmer uses the phrase 'the weight of circumstances' as title for his chapter on 'Irish Fiction', but he does not discuss 'The Ballroom of Romance'.

68. *Stories of William Trevor*, 196.

69. *Stories of William Trevor*, 199.

70. William Trevor, *The Hill Bachelors* (Toronto, 2000), 245. Discussing 'The Ballroom of Romance', Fitzgerald-Hoyt concludes: 'without mawkishness and with respect for Bridie's stoicism and lack of self-pity, Trevor painfully exposes the bleakness of Irish rural life. There are no villains in this story, but simply characters who have no choices, who bravely endure in the face of disappointment ... what might in other hands have been a savage exposure of a narrow life becomes a gentle elegy' (33).

71. Trevor/Stout Interview, 137.

72. *Excursions*, 191.

73. *Excursions*, 25.

74. Some of the ideas presented here were first touched on in my essay '"Bleak Splendour": Notes for an Unwritten Biography of William Trevor', *Colby Quarterly*, 38, 3 (September 2002), 280–94.

4. MAVIS GALLANT'S *GREEN WATER, GREEN SKY*

1. 'Three Brick Walls' and 'Good Morning and Goodbye', *Preview*, 22 (December 1944); 'A Wonderful Country', *The Standard Magazine*, 14 December 1946; and 'The Flowers of Spring', *Northern Review*, 3, 5 (June–July 1950). This last story was rejected by the *New Yorker*, but the story she sent in its place, 'Madeline's Birthday', was published on 1 September 1951; it has been reprinted in Mavis Gallant, *The Cost of Living: Early and Uncollected Stories* (London, 2009, repr. 2010).

2. *Green Water, Green Sky* (Cambridge, Mass., 1959). The 'novel' is divided into four, untitled, parts, three of them corresponding to the stories, although not placed in chronological order. My assumption is that the four parts were written together in 1957/58 in Menton, where Gallant lived for a number of years in the late 1950s. Biographical details are scarce regarding the chronology or circumstances of composition of all Gallant's work; while she provided some details regarding a few stories, in general, she did not, and, indeed, was firm in her insistence that she could not do so. In the case of *Green Water, Green Sky*, there is no documented statement on record.

3. Leslie D. Clement, *Learning to Look: A Visual Response to Mavis Gallant's Fiction* (Montreal and Kingston, 2000), 34. Clement goes on to say, 'The medium of the novel allows Gallant to manipulate and readers to respond to characters in a less enclosed, more open and fluid space than the short

story, with few exceptions, had yet provided', although her argument has less to do with Gallant's use of genre than, more tellingly, about Gallant's interest in the visual arts and how this set of experimental fictions situates the reader in relation to the narrative.

4. The expression 'authentic voice' is taken from 'Voices Lost in Snow', one of the memoir/story sequences written in the mid-1970s. Five of the stories were published in the *New Yorker* in 1976/77 and the set of six was included in *Home Truths: Selected Canadian Stories* (Toronto, 1981). Gallant admitted that the narrator, Linnet Muir, is her most autobiographical creation, and that the reconstructed events probed in these stories correspond closely to two periods in her life, one being her childhood around the age of nine, shortly before her father disappeared. Gallant returned to Montreal alone in 1941 and then lived there until late 1950; four of the stories investigate her young adulthood, the four or five years following her return.

5. According to the Obituary of Gallant in the *New York Times*, 19 February 2014, her father was Stewart de Trafford Young and her mother Benedictine Wiseman, who is referred to as American. In an interview in 2009, Gallant referred to her mother as Canadian.

6. *Selected Stories*, xv.

7. *Selected Stories*, xvi.

8. Obituary, *New York Times*.

9. Interview with Pilar Samacarrera Íñigo, *Atlantis*, 22, 1 (June 2000), 206.

10. Neil K. Besner, *The Light of Imagination: Mavis Gallant's Fiction* (Vancouver, 1988), 54.

11. Interview with Geoff Hancock, *Canadian Fiction Magazine*, 28 (1978), 39.

12. All quotations in this paragraph from *Paris Notebooks*, 233.

13. 'Useless Chaos is What Fiction is About', an interview with Jhumpa Lahiri for *Granta*, 106 (Summer 2009). Accessed online 1 September 2014: <http://granta.com/useless-chaos-is-what-fiction-is-about/>.

14. Hermione Lee, ed., *The Mulberry Tree: Writings of Elizabeth Bowen* (London and New York, 1987), 95–6.

15. *Selected Stories*, xvi–xvii.

16. The idea of writing about a young woman's breakdown appears to have come to Gallant from her experience of 'rooming at school with a girl of fifteen with schizophrenia'. Gallant/Lahiri Interview. Janice Kulyk Keefer remarks that 'the most disconcerting thing about this novel's structure is the disruption of what one assumes will be its central sequence of events'. *Reading Mavis Gallant* (Toronto, 1989), 81. In spite of this apparent frustration with the novel's preoccupation with 'the most fluid of all mediums, time' and that it is 'forever shifting its point of view', Keefer notes that the 'watery world' of Flor's 'unsettled consciousness' is 'appropriately' represented 'in a post-impressionist way' (82).

17. In Besner's excellent comments on the novel, he remarks: '*Green Water, Green Sky* develops through the mirroring effects of a perspective which reflects,

deflects, and refracts the past in character's memories. This mirroring effect is first suggested in the novel's title and then reflected throughout the novel's development' (52). Keefer's detailed reading includes this key observation: 'Though individual characters are shown as being hostile to or clueless about Flor, the narrative voice itself is in almost total sympathy' (81).

18. *Green Water, Green Sky*, 21.
19. *Green Water, Green Sky*, 22–3.
20. *Green Water, Green Sky*, 68–9.
21. *Green Water, Green Sky*, 90.
22. *Green Water, Green Sky*, 111.
23. *Green Water, Green Sky*, 127.
24. *Green Water, Green Sky*, 139.
25. Clement shows that during the 1940s, in Montreal, Gallant became familiar with recent art history and contemporary schools of painting, and even knew personally some of the painters and wrote about them: '[Alfred] Pellan returned to Montreal in 1940 from fourteen years in Paris, where he had been exposed to the cubism of Léger, Picasso and Miro, and the surrealism of Ernst and the later Picasso and Miro. . . . The invigorating controversies that ensued from the formation of two Montreal groups—the Prisme d'Yeux that emerged around Pellan and the more stridently radical Automatistes around [Emile] Borduas—. . . provided a fertile environment for the young Mavis Gallant' (6).
26. *Green Water, Green Sky*, 1.
27. The feeling of abandonment given to George in the opening page is clearly based on Gallant's own experience with her mother at the age of four which she recalled in a number of interviews: 'Three weeks after my fourth birthday I was put in a very, very severe institution. . . . my mother said, "Sit there, and I'll be right back." And she never came back. And that I remember vividly.' Besner, 51.
28. *Green Water, Green Sky*, 20.
29. *Green Water, Green Sky*, 112.
30. *Green Water, Green Sky*, 67.
31. *Green Water, Green Sky*, 29. In the Linnet Muir sequence, the story 'Varieties of Exile' includes the act of writing as a form of exile.
32. *Green Water, Green Sky*, 27–8.
33. *Green Water, Green Sky*, 28.
34. Gallant/Hancock Interview, 46.
35. 'Mavis Gallant: Genesis of a Story', an interview with Kathy Williams, *Aurora*, 1988. Accessed online 24 July 2014: <http://aurora.icaap.org/index.php/aurora/article/view/48/61>.
36. *Selected Stories*, ix.
37. Mavis Gallant, *What is to be done?* (Dunvegan, Ontario, 1983), 61.
38. Gallant/Hancock Interview, 40.
39. Gallant/Lahiri Interview.

40. *Green Water, Green Sky*, 8.
41. *Green Water, Green Sky*, 11.
42. *Green Water, Green Sky*, 11.
43. *Green Water, Green Sky*, 85.
44. Daphne Kalotay, 'The Art of Fiction: Mavis Gallant', *Paris Review*, 153 (Winter 1999). Accessed online 5 September 2014: <http://www.theparis-review.org/interviews/838/the-art-of-fiction-no-160-mavis-gallant>.
45. *Home Truths*, 304.
46. *Home Truths*, 312–13.
47. *Home Truths*, 316.
48. *Home Truths*, 229
49. *Home Truths*, 230.
50. *Home Truths*, 234.
51. *Home Truths*, 235.
52. *Home Truths*, 281.
53. *Home Truths*, 282.
54. *Home Truths*, 282.
55. *Home Truths*, 283.
56. Gallant/Lahiri Interview. Significantly, Karen E. Smythe entitles her discussion of *Green Water, Green Sky* 'The Silent Cry'.
57. *Home Truths*, 293.
58. For a more extended discussion, see Denis Sampson, 'Mavis Gallant's "Voices Lost in Snow": The Origins of Fiction', *Journal of the Short Story in English*, 42 (Spring 2004), 135–45.
59. *Selected Stories*, ix.
60. *Selected Stories*, x.
61. *The Cost of Living*, 196.
62. *The Cost of Living*, 198.
63. *The Cost of Living*, 198–9.
64. *The Cost of Living*, 198.
65. *The Cost of Living*, 201.
66. *Home Truths*, 22.
67. *Home Truths*, 27.
68. Gallant/Kalotay Interview.
69. *The Cost of Living*, 295–6.
70. *The Cost of Living*, 298–9.
71. *The Cost of Living*, 298.
72. *The Cost of Living*, 299.
73. Sandra Martin, 'A Storied Life', *The Globe and Mail*, 6 April 2002.
74. *Green Water, Green Sky*, 135.
75. *Green Water, Green Sky*, 137.
76. *Green Water, Green Sky*, 141.
77. *Green Water, Green Sky*, 146.
78. *Green Water, Green Sky*, 143–4.

79. *Green Water, Green Sky*, 142–3.
80. *Green Water, Green Sky*, 152.
81. *Green Water, Green Sky*, 145.
82. *Green Water, Green Sky*, 143.
83. *Green Water, Green Sky*, 154.
84. Clement also uses 'kaleidoscope' to suggest the kind of fusion of individual identities in George's vision of these 'lost' women in Paris. Her interpretation is situated in a discussion of the movement in the fiction, paralleling certain developments in painting, from two dimensions to four.
85. Interview with Michel Fabre, quoted in Clement, 11.
86. Mavis Gallant, *My Heart is Broken: Eight Stories and a Short Novel* (New York, 1964; repr. Toronto, 1974), 63.
87. *My Heart is Broken*, 154.
88. 'I remember going to Spain [in 1952] . . . it was early spring, but there were just a few trees in bloom. And I thought, this earth is soaked in blood. Spain is soaked in blood, I remember thinking that, the blood of the people who died in that terrible war. And then, thinking it was very dramatic and I was very silly because it is a dramatic thought. It was symbolic.' Gallant/Íñigo Interview, 207.
89. Clement, 11.

5. J. M. COETZEE'S *DUSKLANDS*

1. *Doubling the Point*, 17–18.
2. *Doubling the Point*, 340.
3. 'Homage', 7.
4. 'Homage', 5.
5. *Dusklands* was first published in 1974 in Johannesburg. It did not appear in the UK until 1982 and in the USA until 1985 when it was published in paperback. References here are to the paperback reprint of 1996, 1.
6. David Attwell, *J. M. Coetzee: South Africa and the Politics of Writing* (Berkeley and Los Angeles, 1993) provides a detailed analysis of Coetzee's adaptation of South African sources for 'The Narrative' and American sources for 'The Vietnam Project'.
7. 'Homage', 6.
8. 'Homage', 6.
9. 'Homage', 5.
10. 'Homage', 5.
11. *Dusklands*, 1.
12. *Dusklands*, 1.
13. *Dusklands*, 20.
14. Introduction to Marcellus Emants, *A Posthumous Confession* (1986), included in J. M. Coetzee, *Stranger Shores: Literary Essays, 1986–99* (New York, 2001), 45–6.

15. *Stranger Shores*, 45.
16. *Stranger Shores*, 42.
17. Coetzee's remarks on 'the literary mode of the exhaustive secular confession', in his Introduction to his translation of Emants, are more fully elaborated in an essay which he considered a pivotal point in his development as a critic: 'Confession and Double Thoughts: Rousseau, Tolstoy, Dostoevsky' (1985). The essay is reprinted in *Doubling the Point*. It is evident that soon after this essay, he began to consider how he might write about his boyhood and youth in such a literary context. Derek Attridge, *J. M. Coetzee and the Ethics of Reading: Literature in the Event* (Chicago and London, 2004) has included a very perceptive response to the first two volumes of autobiographical fiction in a chapter entitled 'Confessing in the Third Person'. I have relied guardedly on these confessional volumes for insight into early experiences and responses of the artist.
18. J. M. Coetzee, *Youth* (London, 2002), 137.
19. *Doubling the Point*, 25 and 18. In 1983, Coetzee published his first reflection on his formation, a brief essay entitled 'Remembering Texas', reprinted here.
20. *Doubling the Point*, 19. The details of the various drafts and dates of writing are taken from 'J. M. Coetzee, An Inventory of his Papers at the Harry Ransom Center'. Accessed online 5 December 2013: <http://norman.hrc.utexas.edu/fasearch/findingAid.cfm?eadid=00717>.
21. *Doubling the Point*, 19.
22. *Doubling the Point*, 53.
23. *Doubling the Point*, 65.
24. Carol Clarkson, *J. M. Coetzee: Countervoices* (Basingstoke, 2009), takes this statement as a point of departure for a study that places Coetzee's interest in linguistics at the centre of his artistic achievement. Of interest here is that Clarkson includes a useful discussion of Coetzee's PhD thesis on Beckett's early work, but more generally, her development of insights arising from linguistics and from Bakhtin is extensively perceptive and sympathetic to Coetzee's practice as a writer. Notably, in her Introduction she draws attention to Coetzee's remark that 'Dostoevskian dialogism grows out of Dostoevsky's *own* moral character, out of his ideals, and out of his being as a writer.' This caution leads her to conclude that 'we see in Coetzee an attentiveness and a return to the idea of authorial consciousness—and the ethical implications attendant upon that. These preoccupations constitute a break with more programmatic structuralist conceptions of authorship, authority and authorial consciousness'. Clarkson, 9.
25. *Doubling the Point*, 67.
26. *Doubling the Point*, 67.
27. 'Homage', 7.
28. *Youth*, 61.
29. *Youth*, 62.

30. J. M. Coetzee, *Boyhood: Scenes from Provincial Life* (London, 1998), 7.

31. *Boyhood*, 7.

32. *Boyhood*, 13.

33. *Boyhood*, 124.

34. *Boyhood*, 125.

35. *Boyhood*, 126.

36. Dominic Head, *J. M. Coetzee* (Cambridge and New York, 1997), 29.

37. Dominic Head, *Cambridge Introduction to J. M. Coetzee* (Cambridge, 2009), 42, 38.

38. *Boyhood*, 3.

39. *Boyhood*, 3.

40. *Boyhood*, 3.

41. *Boyhood*, 4.

42. *Boyhood*, 4.

43. *Boyhood*, 4.

44. *Boyhood*, 4.

45. *Boyhood*, 166.

46. Dominic Head includes a far-reaching discussion of this aspect of *Dusklands* in his chapter 'Writing Violence' in his study of 1997, 30–6.

47. *Dusklands*, 96.

48. *Dusklands*, 57.

49. *Dusklands*, 106.

50. *Dusklands*, 107.

51. *Dusklands*, 114.

52. Dominic Head's emphasis on 'the absence of overt authorial judgement' and the ways in which ironies function to create an 'implied authorial judgement' is acute, as is his awareness that a 'self-critique' is central to Coetzee's postmodernist stance.

53. 'Beckett's prose, up to and including *The Unnameable*, has given me a sensuous delight that hasn't dimmed over the years [Coetzee is speaking in 1990]. The critical work I did on Beckett originated in that sensuous response and was a grasping after ways in which to talk about it: to talk about delight.' *Doubling the Point*, 20 and 22.

54. *Youth*, 155.

55. J. M Coetzee, 'The Comedy of Point of View in Beckett's *Murphy*' (1970), repr. in *Doubling the Point*, 36.

56. *Doubling the Point*, 37.

57. *Doubling the Point*, 42.

58. *Doubling the Point*, 47.

59. J. M. Coetzee, 'The Manuscript Revisions of Beckett's *Watt*' (1972), repr. in *Doubling the Point*, 39.

60. *Doubling the Point*, 37.

61. *Doubling the Point*, 43–4.

62. *Doubling the Point*, 23.

63. *Doubling the Point*, 25.
64. *Doubling the Point*, 27.
65. Kannemeyer, 234. Kannemeyer notes that the translation was completed before Coetzee left the United States in May 1971, that it was accepted for publication in 1973, and appeared in 'The Library of Netherlandic Literature' in 1975.
66. 'Homage', 7.
67. 'Homage', 5.
68. Kannemeyer, 175.
69. 'Homage', 5.
70. 'Homage', 5.
71. 'Homage', 5. Surprisingly, Coetzee does not note the fact that it was the overshadowing presence of Hiberno-English, English as spoken in Ireland, that Beckett wished to modify by writing in French. In relation to this, a further quotation from 'Homage' may be enlightening: 'The lesson is not so much about getting the movements of the voice onto the page as about finding a form for the movements of the mind' (6).
72. Kannemeyer, 182.
73. Kannemeyer, 183.
74. Kannemeyer, 182.
75. *Dusklands*, vii.
76. *Dusklands*, 46.
77. *Dusklands*, 37.
78. *Doubling the Point*, 393–4.
79. *Doubling the Point*, 392. In addition to using the word 'grace' to refer to the truth a literary artist may tell, he also refers to the 'analytic intensity' of reading the work of other artists, such as Kafka, as a kind of 'grace' (199).
80. *Doubling the Point*, 341.
81. J. M. Coetzee, *White Writing: On the Culture of Letters in South Africa* (New Haven and London, 1988), 38.
82. *White Writing*, 38.
83. *Youth*, 137.
84. *Boyhood*, 80.
85. *Boyhood*, 81.
86. *Boyhood*, 79.
87. *Boyhood*, 50.
88. J. M. Coetzee, *Summertime: Fiction* (New York, 2009), 97.
89. *Boyhood*, 95.
90. *Stranger Shores*, 7.
91. *Stranger Shores*, 6.
92. *Stranger Shores*, 6–7. The complete title of *Boyhood* is *Boyhood: Scenes from a Provincial Life*, and in one edition, *Youth* is entitled *Youth: Scenes from Provincial Life II*; these two works and *Summertime: Fiction* appeared together in one volume, *Scenes from Provincial Life*, in 2011.

93. *Stranger Shores*, 8–9.
94. *Stranger Shores*, 13.
95. *Stranger Shores*, 16.
96. *Summertime*, 61.

EPILOGUE: 'WRITER AS WRITER'

1. *Literary Occasions*, 194.
2. The allusion here is to William Golding's novel *The Paper Men*, in which he studies an author who is harassed by a would-be biographer.
3. Eudora Welty, *One Writer's Beginnings* (London, 1985), 99–100.
4. *One Writer's Beginnings*, 101.

Index

Coetzee, J.M. (*cont.*)
  Hears Bach, embraces the idea of
    classic art, 139–41
  'Homage', 149n, 163n, 164n, 166n
  Karoo, family farm, 135–9
  Leaves Capetown for London,
    works as computer
    programmer, 115
  Mother (Vera Wehmeyer),
    123–6, 143
  Moves to Texas for graduate
    studies, Buffalo for teaching
    position, 116–17
  Returns to Capetown, due to
    anti-Vietnam War protests,
    135–9
  Stranger Shores: Literary Essays,
    163n, 164n, 166n, 167n
  Summertime: Fiction, 114, 138,
    141–2, 166n, 167n
  University studies in literature
    and mathematics, 115
  White Writing, 166n
  Youth, 114, 116, 139, 141
colonialism, 8, 13, 14, 17, 21–2,
  27–8
confession as a literary genre, 111–2,
  113–15, 130, 132, 137, 142
cultural inheritance, 4, 5, 10, 13, 18,
  22, 46–7, 56, 60, 61, 65, 68,
  71–2, 83, 112, 115, 123

Descartes, René, 114
Dickens, Charles, 10, 20, 24, 54, 56,
  60, 62
Dostoevsky, Fyodor, 115, 130,
  132, 141

Eliot, T.S., 113, 115, 139–41, 157n
Emants, Marcellus, 115, 130
  Posthumous Confession, A, (trans
    J.M. Coetzee), 115, 130
estrangement, 4, 13–14, 18–19, 33, 35,
  96, 107, 130–1
  and exile, 25, 27, 91, 92–3, 95, 98,
    110, 137

Flaubert, Gustave, 25, 128, 139
Forster, E.M., 70, 157n
Freud, Sigmund, 84

Gallant, Mavis, née Young,
  Childhood in Montreal (b.1922),
    81, 96–8, 100–1
  *Cost of Living: Early and Uncollected
    Stories, The*, 100–3,
    159n, 162n
  'Rose', 100–2
  'Wedding Ring, The', 101, 103
  Collapse of family (age 10),
    Gallant placed with
    guardians, 82
  Father (Stewart Young), 82, 83,
    97–100, 105
  First writing, 92
  French, language of boarding
    school, 81
  Green Water, Green Sky, 80, 81,
    82, 85, 86–92, 95, 98, 101,
    103, 106–9, 159n, 160n,
    161n, 162n
  *Home Truths: Selected Canadian
    Stories*, 83, 96–100,
    160n, 162n
    'Doctor, The', 96–7
    'Jorinda and Jorindel', 101,
      102–3
    'Voices Lost in Snow',
      99–100, 160n
    'In Youth is Pleasure', 97
  Leaves Montreal for Europe,
    nomadic for a decade, 82
  Marxist political commitment, 83
  Mother (Benedictine Wiseman),
    103–5
  My Heart is Broken, 103, 109, 163n
  'Its Image on the Mirror',
    103, 109
  New York, liberation, 84
  Other Paris, The, 90
  *Paris Notebooks: Essays and
    Reviews*, 149n
  'What is Style?' 149n